GHOSTHUNTING
PENNSYLVANIA

AMERICA'S
HAUNTED ROAD TRIP

Titles in the *America's Haunted Road Trip* Series:

GHOSTHUNTING PENNSYLVANIA

ROSEMARY ELLEN GUILEY

CLERISY PRESS

Ghosthunting Pennsylvania

Published by Clerisy Press
Distributed by Publishers Group West
Printed in the United States of America
First edition, third printing 2016

Library of Congress Cataloging-in-Publication Data
    Guiley, Rosemary.
        Ghosthunting Pennsylvania / Rosemary Ellen Guiley.
            p. cm.
        Includes bibliographical references.
        ISBN-13: 978-1-57860-353-4
        ISBN-10: 1-57860-353-6
        1. Ghosts—Pennsylvania. 2. Haunted places—Pennsylvania.
        I. Title.

        BF1472.U6G85 2009
        133.109748—dc22

                                                    2009034264

Editor: John Kachuba
Cover design: Scott McGrew
Cover and interior photos provided by Rosemary Ellen Guiley

Clerisy Press
306 Greenup Street
Covington, KY 41011
www.clerisypress.com

TABLE OF CONTENTS

CENTRAL PENNSYLVANIA 43

SOUTHERN PENNSYLVANIA 79

NORTHERN PENNSYLVANIA 185

Welcome to America's Haunted Road Trip

DO YOU BELIEVE IN GHOSTS?

If you are like 52 percent of Americans (according to a recent Harris Poll), you *do* believe that ghosts walk among us. Perhaps you have heard your name called in a dark and empty house. It could be that you have awoken to the sound of footsteps outside your bedroom door, only to find no one there. It is possible that you saw your grandmother sitting in her favorite rocker chair, the same grandmother who had passed away several years before. Maybe you took a photo of a crumbling, deserted farmhouse and discovered strange mists and orbs in the photo, anomalies that were not visible to your naked eye.

If you have experienced similar paranormal events, then you know that ghosts exist. Even if you have not yet experienced these things, you are curious about the paranormal world, the spirit realm. If you weren't, you would not now be reading this preface to the latest book in the *America's Haunted Road Trip* series from Clerisy Press.

Over the last several years, I have investigated haunted locations across the country, and with each new site, I found myself becoming more fascinated with ghosts. What are they? How do they manifest themselves? Why are they here? These are just a few of the questions I have been asking. No doubt, you have been asking the same questions.

The books in the *America's Haunted Road Trip* series can help you find the answers to your questions about ghosts. We've gathered together some of America's top ghost writers (no pun intended) and researchers and asked them to write about their states' favorite haunts. Each location that they write about is open to the public so that you can visit them for yourself and try out your ghosthunting skills. In addition to telling you about their often hair-raising adventures, the writers have included maps and travel directions so that you can take your own haunted road trip.

In this addition to the series, *Ghosthunting Pennsylvania*, well-known paranormal researcher Rosemary Ellen Guiley shines her spotlight on the ghostly denizens of the Keystone State. The book is a spine-tingling trip through Pennsylvania's small towns and cosmopolitan cities, from the streets of eighteenth-century Philadelphia to the Allegheny Mountain towns founded on coal mining. Ride shotgun with Rosemary as she seeks out Civil War ghosts at Gettysburg and the Cashtown Inn, or the ghosts of murdered Indians at—of all the unlikely places—the Fulton Opera House in Lancaster. Travel with her to the Hotel Conneaut where a ghost named Elizabeth still flees the fire that took her life, or to the Carbon County Jail where the ghosts of several hanged "Molly Maguires" still hang around and where one of them has left a handprint that cannot be erased. And can there really be ghosts in Pittsburgh's National Aviary? Hang on tight; *Ghosthunting Pennsylvania* is a scary ride.

But once you've finished reading this book, don't unbuckle your seatbelt. There are still forty-nine states left for your haunted road trip! See you on the road!

John Kachuba
Editor, America's Haunted Road Trip

Introduction

PENNSYLVANIA TRULY RANKS as one of the most haunted states in America. For the past fifteen or so years, it has been my second home in my full-time travels and investigations of the paranormal. I've visited many haunted places around the country and even around the world, and I have always considered Pennsylvania to be one of the richest in ghostly lore and phenomena.

Why is Pennsylvania so extraordinarily haunted? It is a big state, but size is not necessarily the reason. Pennsylvania has an amazing diversity of history, cultures, personalities, industry, arts, and terrain, all contributing to a colorful haunted heritage. It was already a multicultural melting pot in precolonial days thanks to the mapping, explorations, and settlements of the Europeans and English. Pennsylvania and its citizens played prominent roles in the Revolutionary War and the formation of the United States of America. Numerous battles were fought on her soil, most notably the French and Indian War, Revolutionary War, and the Civil War. In fact, the pivotal battle of the Civil War was fought in Gettysburg, Pennsylvania. The blood that was shed there determined the future of the United States.

Pennsylvania hauntings also have been shaped by the mining, river transportation, railroads, and iron and steel works that brought thousands of immigrants to the state, especially in the 1700s and 1800s. In a short period of time, dozens of cultures were transplanted with their folk beliefs, superstitions and haunted lore.

No one knows for certain why any place becomes haunted, but researchers over the last century or so have arrived at a few explanations that seem likely, based on patterns of experience. Traumatic events, especially unhappy and violent ones, are the leading candidates for hauntings. War, battles, accidents, crimes, and emotionally traumatic events have a way of etching themselves onto the fabric of time and space so that they linger for future generations to notice. Strangely, happy events don't seem to have the same power. And a negative event does not necessarily guarantee a haunting. I have investigated some places where horrific crimes were committed and people died horribly, yet the places themselves are poorly haunted at best.

Many people believe that dying or being buried at a location will make it haunted. There are plenty of candidates to support that belief, but actually it is not necessarily always the case. Plenty of places are haunted that have no records of deaths taking place there. And if burial places were automatically haunted, then every cemetery would be filled with ghosts. Instead, most paranormal investigators find cemeteries to be some of the worst candidates for hauntings.

Sometimes places seem haunted because of memories—they were favorites of the ghosts when they were living. Most of these hauntings are "residuals" or "imprints"—they are psychic memories that have no intelligence. The ghosts do the same things in the same places, like broken records or video loops.

I believe that the living participate in hauntings, probably unwittingly. Collectively, we have our favorite time periods, events in history and historical personalities. We are mesmerized by certain events, such as battles fought in a war, or a love story gone bad involving high-profile people of historical importance. I have long believed that such interest helps to fuel some hauntings, thus giving us a vicarious way of participating in past events.

Finally, perhaps one of the most important factors of all is the energy of the place. The earth is filled with fluctuations in electromagnetic energy due to topography, minerals, soil content, mining tunnels, large bodies of water, and running water. Researchers believe that it is no accident that hot spots at hauntings and other paranormal phenomena occur in areas where there are high concentrations of quartz, mica, magnetite, and iron, as well as huge lakes and large rivers. Some highly haunted places sit on negative magnetic anomalies. These natural earth forces may bend space and time in such a way that we can experience the past through hauntings. Pennsylvania is full of places with those kinds of earth energy signatures.

Thus, a place may be haunted because of a unique convergence of factors, with no two sites being haunted in exactly the same way and for the same reasons. Finding out the activity and the possible causes for it, and trying to document evidence of the activity, are the reasons why so many people are attracted to the paranormal and decide to investigate it.

In my full-time work in the paranormal, I am always in search of good evidence of hauntings. Despite a century or more of documented "evidence in support of" ghosts and hauntings, we still do not have conclusive proof that would satisfy scientists. Nonetheless, just about everyone has been haunted at some point, and cannot deny the experience. Do ghosts exist? I am firmly convinced that they do, based on my years of research, documentation, and most importantly, my personal experiences. I have seen apparitions, felt invisible presences, heard disembodied voices, and witnessed the unexplained movements of objects. The haunted places in the book are famous for such phenomena, and many people experience the same things at the same locations.

You don't have to be a researcher to experience the paranormal, however. Many of the stories in this book come from people who were not looking for ghosts when the ghosts found them. Pennsylvania's haunted places can be enjoyed casually, in the spirit of vacations and getaways that have an extra thrill to them. Whenever I travel, I always look for a haunted hotel, inn, or restaurant, as well as other places that have mystery to their history. There is no guarantee of experiencing phenomena, for ghosts are capricious and do not perform on demand. But if you travel the paranormal roads enough, the odds are very good that you will be haunted!

Rosemary Ellen Guiley

EASTERN
PENNSYLVANIA

Bethlehem
  Hotel Bethlehem
Levittown
  Bolton Mansion
New Hope
  Logan Inn

Philadelphia
  Eastern State Penitentiary
  Fort Mifflin
Riegelsville
  Riegelsville Inn

CHAPTER 1

Hotel Bethlehem

Bethlehem

ONE OF THE BIGGEST PARANORMAL hot spots in Pennsylvania is in the Bethlehem area in the Lehigh Valley, and Hotel Bethlehem ranks as the number one ghost destination. Large, stately and elegant, the hotel anchors the town's historic district, steeped in the culture of the founding Moravians. It is full of ghostly activity.

The hotel's site was originally occupied by Bethlehem's very first house, built by the founding Moravians in 1741. As commerce grew, the Moravian Church tore down the house and built the Eagle Hotel on the site. The Eagle served as an adjunct to the nearby Sun Inn, which could overflow with guests. In the early twentieth century, the Eagle was demolished, and in 1920 financial businessman Charles Schwab built Hotel Bethlehem on the site. Schwab wanted an elegant place to impress all his high-profile clients.

Since then, the hotel has changed ownership three more times. The present owners are still doing extensive renovating to restore it to its original grandeur. Hotel Bethlehem is one of only 213 hotels and resorts that are members of the National Trust Historic Hotels of America, a program of the National Trust for Historic Preservation.

The hotel teems with ghosts. Numerous guests report the same or similar experiences in certain rooms and areas. The hotel also is popular with paranormal investigators.

Natalie Bock, the hotel's special events manager and historian, took me on an extensive tour to acquaint me with the range of activity. Every hotel has its "most haunted" room or rooms, and at the Hotel Bethlehem the winner is Room 932. An apparition of a man appears at the bedside in the middle of the night. One couple described him as wearing an undershirt and boxer shorts. He vanished when they turned on the light. The couple was so unnerved that they checked out that night.

Another couple was awakened by the ghostly man, who asked them why they were in his room. He also vanished when the light was turned on.

A woman staying in Room 932 went into the bathroom, turned on the light, and saw an entirely different room, one with pink wallpaper. Perhaps, she saw a glimpse of the room as it had been in the past.

Other guests have reported that they saw papers fly off the desk and lights blink on and off. There are photos of the room in which orbs appear.

Room 932 may be the hotel's most famous haunted guest room, but Bock says many of the other rooms also have ghostly activity. Plumbing turns off and on without explanation, other apparitions are seen, phantom voices are heard, and objects are moved about.

Among the ghostly residents are several that stand out for their frequent appearances and details:

– Francis "Daddy" Thomas welcomed and attended to visitors who came to Bethlehem. He was known for his kindness and humor. His ghost has been sighted in the boiler room area.

– Mrs. Brong was an innkeeper of the old Eagle Hotel with her husband until they were fired by the Moravian Church in 1833. The Church officials were mortified by their unacceptable and outrageous behavior. Mr. Brong liked to get so drunk that he had to be laid out on a bench. Mrs. Brong shocked guests by going barefoot while she worked. Mr. Brong has not lingered, but Mrs. Brong is seen by staff and guests in the restaurant and kitchen, dressed in attire of the 1800s. Still defiant of the propriety of her era, she wears no shoes or stockings.

– Mary "May" Yohe was born at the old Eagle Hotel in 1866 and was still a child when she danced and sang for the hotel guests in the lobby. The Moravians sent her to Paris to learn opera. By 1888, she was famous on stage for her singing and dancing, and off stage for her torrid romances. During the 1890s, she went to England and fell in love with Lord Francis Clinton Hope, whom she married. Hope owned the infamous Hope Diamond, a large and rare blue diamond that was named for the family and reputed to be cursed. Mary often wore the gem. Did it doom her marriage? Something did, for

May left Hope for an American soldier, who later
turned the tables and left her. May's ghost sings,
and the player piano in the lounge frequently plays
on its own.

May is thought to be the ghost of a little girl seen in the exercise room on the third floor, and also in the lobby.

The exercise room on the third floor has mysterious activity in addition to May. No one is in it late at night, but guests on the fourth floor will complain of noises coming from below, as though someone is working the equipment. The figure of a little girl, believed to be May, has been seen in the window by an engineer who was closing up for the night. Another guest wandered up from an evening wedding party and saw a little girl on the equipment. He warned her to get off, not realizing he was talking to a ghost.

The sounds of weights being dropped may be due to another ghost reported on the third floor, that of a former employee named Frank Smith. Smith had some financial dealings that went bad. One day his secretary came in and found his suit jacket neatly folded over his office chair. Smith was nowhere to be seen, nor did he turn up as the day went on. Finally, the secretary had to make a photocopy, and went to the restroom where the copy machine stood. The door refused to budge. She summoned help, and soon a grisly discovery was made—Smith's body had fallen against the inside of the door. From appearances, he had committed suicide by shooting himself twice with a .357 magnum, once in the leg and once in the head. According to forensics expert Katherine Ramsland, it is unusual for suicide victims to shoot themselves twice, but not unheard of. Smith may have shot himself in the leg hoping to bleed to death, and then decided to do the job once and for all.

Smith's widow went to court to try to collect on his insurance policy, but lost, because his death was ruled a suicide, not an accident or crime. His ghost appears as a man in a suit and has startled the hotel staff.

Stand in the lobby late at night, and you might notice the elevators coming to the first floor uncalled. You might also feel watched or see shadowy figures walking about, especially along the railing of the balcony above the lobby.

In the kitchen, a previous chef found himself kicked by an invisible presence—perhaps the ghost wanted a meal!

Down in the basement, massive boilers heat the hotel. A dark shadowy figure of a man wearing a triangular hat is frequently seen flitting about by staff, especially in the wee hours of the night. The figure is spooky and moves very fast, sometimes tapping people on the shoulder. He makes many employees uncomfortable. The ghost never leaves the basement. He is believed to be a man from colonial times, possibly one of the early Moravian settlers.

In administrative office areas, staff have heard whistling and seen the window blinds move by themselves as though someone is walking rapidly by. Objects on desks have been seen moving by themselves. Shadowy figures show up on the screens.

Other phenomena can be experienced throughout the hotel. The third floor has cold spots and unaccountable breezes. On the mezzanine, a guest once felt the presence of a sad girl about three years old, dressed in white peering through the mezzanine's railing. Others heard a child playing in halls and sighted a young girl dressed in white.

Hotel Bethlehem is proud of its heritage, both historical and ghostly. Add to that its elegant ambience, finely appointed rooms, and superb dining, and you have an all-in-one haunted vacation.

Spotlight on Ghosts:
Do Not Disturb the Dead at God's Acre

Nestled in downtown historic Bethlehem is a serene, tree-protected Moravian cemetery dating to the eighteenth century. Neat rows of hundreds of graves, all marked by flat white marble headstones, line the grassy ground. If they look like a garden of the dead, it is no accident. The Moravians, who came to America from Germany, called many of their cemeteries "God's Acre" in the notion that the dead are planted, awaiting to spring into new life at the coming of Christ.

The flat headstones are neat and of similar size, for the Moravians also believed in equality in death as well as in life. They prohibited the erection of large, showy headstones.

The God's Acre in Bethlehem was established in 1748. Mohicans are buried here among the Moravians, including the chief who was the historical basis for Uncas in James Fenimore Cooper's famous novel, *The Last of the Mohicans.* His real name was Tschoop, and he was from Dutchess County, New York. Tschoop, who took the Anglicized name John, died of smallpox in an epidemic that claimed many lives.

The Moravians were dedicated diary keepers, and it is believed that Cooper got his inspiration for the novel by reading some of the diaries about the Mohicans.

God's Acre is a peaceful place, and it seems the dead want to keep it that way. On one occasion, investigators Katherine Ramsland and Rick Fisher visited to collect EVP. They asked if anyone in the cemetery wished to communicate, and Ramsland recorded a voice that answered, "Why are you doing this to us?" as though they were disturbing the peace of the dead.

On another occasion Fisher visited and recorded a tour of the cemetery led by Natalie Bock, the historian of the Bethlehem Hotel. He discovered he had captured an unknown woman's voice superimposed on top of Bock's voice. The unknown voice said loudly and firmly, "Leave, *please.*"

CHAPTER 2

Bolton Mansion

LEVITTOWN

BOLTON MANSION IS REMINISCENT of stately homes found in England and comes with English-style hauntings as well. The mansion was built by the Phineas Pemberton family in 1687 on a five-hundred-acre estate, and was named after their home in Bouton, Lancashire, England. The name became Americanized to "Bolton." Today, the town it is located in is known as Levittown in Bucks County. The house is one of the most significant in Pennsylvania, not only from an architectural standpoint, but from an historical standpoint as well. Nearly all of its inhabitants since the days of William Penn have influenced the course of history in the state.

Pemberton, a grocer, came to America with his family in 1682, sailing on the ship *Submission* from Liverpool. Besides his wife Phoebe, he brought his two children and his parents. They landed at Choptank, Maryland. They made their way to Pennsylvania, where Pemberton bought three hundred acres of land and built a small house called Grove Place. It proved to be too damp and inhospitable, and so he soon built the mansion on another site. He became the first clerk of the Bucks County courts, a post he held until his death in 1702. William Penn said upon news of Pemberton's passing, "I will mourn for poor Phineas Pemberton, the ablest, as well as one of the best men in the province."

Bolton Mansion was expanded and renovated several times up to the middle of the nineteenth century, giving it a mixed personality of designs in its twenty-seven rooms. Phineas's son, Israel, added substantially to it when he inherited it upon his father's death in 1702. Subsequent generations of Pembertons gave the house their own embellishments.

In 1938 it was given to the University of Pennsylvania, which had used the property as an experimental farm as early as the 1820s. After that, various owners held the property until Bristol Township purchased it for use as a municipal building, abandoning the building in 1966. The home then sat vacant for several decades. It is now a National Historic Landmark managed by the Bucks County Conservancy.

Bolton Mansion has several resident ghosts. One is a lady in a long dress and cloak who roams the grounds at night. She is seen surrounded by an aura of glowing light. Another ghost is a woman who also walks the grounds, crying to herself as she searches for someone. Perhaps she is searching for the little girl whose ghost lives on the second floor and runs from window to window. She is glimpsed looking out as though she, too, is searching for someone.

The most famous phantoms are a Confederate soldier and his sweetheart. According to lore, the soldier was the son of the owner of the estate during the Civil War. He fell in love with a servant girl, Mary. Pennsylvania was part of the Union, but the young man enlisted in the army to fight for the South. His angry father disowned him.

When the war ended, the son returned home, but his father refused to forgive him. The rejection was too much for the young man, who was undoubtedly traumatized by the war. He hung himself from the second floor stairwell. His body was found by Mary, who was so overcome with grief that she shot herself. Another version says she hung herself from the stairs. Their misty figures have been seen going up the stairs. Volunteers at the mansion report hearing phantom screams and moans at the bottom and top of the main stairs.

A woman's misty form moves between the barn outbuilding and the east side of the house. She appears to be looking for something or somebody, and is always in a hurry, rushing back and forth. A glowing form has been seen on the front lawn.

A ghostly little girl roams about the third floor of the mansion. Her name and historical identity are not known.

The ghost of a man has been reported in the attic.

In 1977, a professor took infrared photos inside the mansion. One shows a figure resembling a woman in a hoop skirt, and another shows what appears to be the profile of a man wearing pants with a stripe down the side.

The mansion has a schedule of weekend openings to the public. Some paranormal groups have investigated there. One group, the Garden State Ghost Hunter Society (GSGHS), founded by Boni Bates, collected interesting data on two investigations. They sought to establish communication with one of the ghosts with a K2 meter, which measures fluctuations in electromagnetic energy. The fluctuations register in flashing lights. Many investigators believe that spirits can communicate by causing the lights to flash.

The team established communication with a female entity who said she thought the time period was the 1790s. When asked to make a banging sound, she complied. The energy faded after about an hour, which is typical for these types of alleged spirit communications. They also used the meter to communicate with two children spirits who said they were in the fireplace hiding from a man.

The investigators heard heavy footsteps in areas where no one was present, and saw shadows moving about inside the house. They collected a number of EVP recordings, including voices that said "yes," "careful," and "do you want to be friends with me?" Other EVPs were of a door slamming shut and the guitar being played.

Bates, who is mediumistic, had an encounter with a shadowy figure in the basement. "I'm able to see the energy around me," she said. "You know how a car engine looks in the summer time with waves of heat coming off it? That's how I see spirit energy. It is darker than the room itself. I can feel it, too. On one of our investigations, I felt myself being pulled to go down to the basement. As soon as I hit the bottom steps, I saw the outline of a dark figure, bigger than me. I was startled and called out to my husband, 'Hey Rob!' As soon as I said that, it started moving back through the walls. I said, 'No, come back, come back.' But it disappeared. That's the way it goes!"

CHAPTER 3

Logan Inn
NEW HOPE

NEW HOPE, located on the Delaware River in Bucks County northwest of Philadelphia, has long had the reputation of being one of the most haunted towns in America. And the Colonial-era Logan Inn ranks at the top of New Hope's list of "most haunted."

The Logan Inn was built in 1727 by John Wells, who is also credited with founding the town of New Hope. Wells had a license to run a ferry and constructed the inn around his ferry service. In those days, the town was known as Coryell's Ferry, and it became famous as an important stopover in travel. During the Revolutionary War, General George Washington and his men wintered near there one year.

Most of the citizens made their living at the local mills, but in 1790 disaster struck when the mills burned. The mills were rebuilt and the town changed its name to reflect its spirit of determined optimism—New Hope.

After the turn of the twentieth century, the town went into decline and struggled to find a new identity. It succeeded in becoming a center for artists and a tourist attraction. Today the streets are jammed with visitors who come to take in the quaint ambience, stroll the riverbank, shop, and enjoy meals in the many fine restaurants. The Bucks County Playhouse is a major attraction.

The Logan Inn was originally known as the Ferry Tavern. It was purchased by a resident named Abraham Meyers, who renamed it after James Logan, secretary to William Penn, in 1828. Logan had exchanged names with the chief of the Lenni-Lanape Indians as an act of good faith and brotherhood, and Meyers admired him. He had a weathervane of the renamed Chief Logan made for the tavern.

According to lore, a curse of sorts haunts the inn: if the weathervane is ever removed, the inn will be destroyed by fire. The legend originated about sixty years ago when the weathervane fell down in a storm. The owner at the time put it in the barn, which caught fire the same night. Everything was destroyed except for the weathervane. In the 1970s, Carl Lutz, owner of the inn at that time, put the vane up on a new post. The inn has done well ever since. It now ranks as the oldest continually run inn in Bucks County, and one of five of the oldest such inns in the United States.

The Logan Inn features sixteen rooms, all elegantly furnished in colonial decor and antiques. A restaurant serves up traditional American fare. Guests come and go, but several ghostly residents live full-time at the inn, and many visitors have been experienced them. At least one ghost stomps around with the heavy sound of boots.

If you book a room at the Logan, ask for Room 6, also called Emily's Room, the most active in terms of hauntings. Despite its corner location, the room often has an unexplained chill. Named after Emily Lutz, the mother of Carl Lutz, the corner room overlooks both Main and Ferry streets. Emily lived here and died of natural causes in her late eighties. Some of her original furniture, including an armoire, is still in the room. So is Emily, and she likes to look in on guests. People smell her lavender perfume in the room and also near her portrait that hangs in the lobby. The large painting of Emily and her husband, Charles Lutz, shows them with lavender sprigs.

Emily's glowing ghost is seen by some guests. She likes to adjust the heat in the room. Some guests leave the room and return to find their luggage relocated to a different spot. Others find small objects mysteriously knocked off tables. Guests have felt light touches at night, and some say their pillows are pulled out from beneath their heads. Others hear the sounds of a woman crying in the room.

One story goes that a businessman who slept in the room woke up feeling pressure on his chest. Looking up, he was startled to see a white, misty shape in the room. He left immediately, even though it was the middle of the night.

Emily wanders throughout the inn and has been spotted in the dining room downstairs. One of the local shopkeepers told me, "I was having dinner there one night with my husband. I got up to go to the ladies' room, and out of the corner of my eye I saw a woman wearing a long, old-fashioned dress. I turned and looked directly at her, and she disappeared. I thought it was my imagination. I must have looked startled, because a girl who worked on the staff asked me if I was okay. I told her what I had seen, and she nodded and said that I'd probably seen Emily."

Keep an eye on the mirror in Emily's Room. Mirrors have a long-standing reputation in folklore to be doorways to the unknown. The ghostly reflection of a tearful man is seen in the mirror, especially in dim light at night. In addition, the ghosts of two children, whose identities are not known, have been seen in the room and in the mirror. One of them may also be the ghost of a little girl seen in the parking lot. She is believed to be a girl who drowned after falling off a bridge.

The ghost of an unknown Revolutionary War soldier is seen wandering throughout the Inn, especially in the bar—the oldest part of the tavern—dining room, and basement. He sometimes stands as though he is waiting for something. To some witnesses, he looks solid and real, like a person dressed in costume. But he vanishes unexpectedly and leaves cold air behind him. He is believed to be the ghost of one of the soldiers whose bodies were stored in the basement. During the war, many troops passed through New Hope, and a fair number died from illness, disease, and the cold. The frozen winter ground outside was too hard for burials. The bodies were stored in the tavern basement until they could be cremated.

A headless Revolutionary War soldier has also been seen on the second floor.

Another male ghost, dressed in colonial breeches, has been seen near the men's restroom and in the basement. This ghost may be responsible for the sounds of heavy footsteps, the turning on and off of lights, and the inexplicable tumbling of beer kegs, all in the basement.

Aaron Burr is said to have stayed at the inn after his famous duel in which he killed Alexander Hamilton. His ghost is rumored to appear on the premises.

My stay at the Logan was cozy. I was able to get Room 5, next to Emily's room, anchored by an impressive four-poster bed. I ate in the tavern and talked to several regulars, one of whom said that, on occasion, he had seen what might be ghosts. "I've never known for sure," he said. "You look and they're gone."

Late at night trails of lavender scent wafted down the hall upstairs where the lodging rooms are. I looked out my door, but the hallway was empty, and all the rooms seemed quiet.

The ghosts at the Logan are amiable. The inn lends an air of comfort and ease, and the ghosts fit right in.

Spotlight on Ghosts: Porches

There are plenty of haunted places off the beaten "ghost track" in New Hope. One of them is Porches, a cozy and comfortable bed-and-breakfast tucked away on Fisher's Alley, fronting the Delaware River towpath and right in the center of town. Porches is a favorite of Adele Gamble, who leads the town's ghost tour.

The home was built in 1815 as a granary and it served as a hiding place for the Underground Railroad prior to the Civil War. The present owner and proprietor, John, purchased the property around 2000. A friend of his, Tommy, had lived there his entire life, and had passed away in 1995. Tommy loved to sit out on his porch on pleasant days and evenings. It is his ghost that some think is seen and felt on the premises, still visiting his beloved home.

When John renovated the place into a bed-and-breakfast, he had the old porch taken down. During the renovation, a psychic who visited told John that Tommy was unhappy about not having a porch. John said to assure him that a new porch would be built, and Tommy would have all the porch space he wanted. Porches now wrap around the house on both ground and upper levels and are furnished with wicker chairs and tables for breakfast and relaxing.

Tommy is experienced mostly in the living room, which serves as a lounge and entertainment center; the dining room; and Room 2. Gamble has stayed in Room 2. While relaxing in the easy chair, she caught a glimpse of a male figure walking past her.

John's cat, Spencer, loves to greet guests and tag along to their rooms. John has seen a phantom cat in the house as well.

The atmosphere at Porches is laid back and comfortable. John is a congenial host who wants his guests to feel at home. Apparently Tommy feels the same way, still enjoying the ambience along with the guests.

CHAPTER 4

Eastern State Penitentiary
PHILADELPHIA

THE QUAKERS WHO SETTLED in Pennsylvania in colonial days thought they had the right solution to crime and punishment. Time spent sitting in a jail cell was wasted unless prisoners were made fit to rejoin society. The founders of Eastern State Penitentiary created a unique penal and rehabilitation system that they thought could not fail. But it did, spectacularly. What happened at the prison undoubtedly made it one of the most weirdly haunted jails in the country.

Eastern State Penitentiary makes an imposing cut in the Philadelphia skyline, a giant granite fortress with forbidding walls, covering eleven acres in the Fairmount section of town. No longer a working prison, Eastern State is a historic site that draws thousands of visitors every year. Some come to see the cells where famous killers and gangsters, such as Al Capone, were housed. Many of the visitors are ghosthunters and paranormal investigators who hope to experience the vivid phantom sounds and sights of prisoners long dead. Few people depart disappointed.

I have visited and conducted all-night paranormal investigations at Eastern State four times. The site is quite active with a wide variety of phenomena. The how and why of these hauntings were shaped by the prison's unusual history.

Eastern State opened in 1829, hailed as a revolutionary prison. Architects competed to win the privilege of designing it. The winner was John Haviland, an Englishman who had immigrated to America and settled in Philadelphia. Haviland created a design never before used in a prison. Within the rectangular fortress walls is a flower with eight petals. Each petal holds a long row of cells. At the center of the flower is the guard command center. Mirrors were positioned so that a guard could easily look down any petal and see whether the inmates were behaving. The design was an innovative monitoring system that inspired imitation by at least three hundred other prisons.

Most revolutionary of all was the treatment of inmates, who included women as well as men. The Quakers were accustomed to spending long periods of silence in prayer and contemplation. They reasoned that prisoners would benefit from the same. Other prisons had experimented with forced silence during certain periods and activities, such as eating and recreation, but the Quakers took it to the extreme. If prisoners were forced to spend their jail time in total isolation, cut off from even seeing another human face, they would have to turn inward to think deeply about their crimes and how they would reform themselves. They would become penitent, that is, sad and regretful about having done wrong, and serving a penance as a consequence.

In fact, the Quakers' emphasis on becoming penitent gave rise to the word "penitentiary" to describe prisons.

The Quakers and others had a great deal of confidence in this approach to rehabilitation. "If reform can happen . . . it will happen here" was said about the new system.

It seemed like a noble idea, but it backfired horribly. Inmates were never allowed to see each other, or even guards. There were no communal workouts—each cell had a private yard for exercise, with high walls that prevented contact with neighboring inmates. There were no communal meals. Instead, food was slid through slits in the solid cell doors. If inmates had to be moved, hoods were put over their heads. They were not allowed to talk to anyone.

Additional brutalities and cruelties were heaped upon prisoners. Inmates were punished in barbaric ways, such as being chained and strapped into uncomfortable positions on chairs for long periods, and being soaked with water and then chained to walls while the water froze on their clothing and skin. Inmates who broke the no-talking rule were painfully bound and gagged with the Iron Gag, a bridle placed in their mouths and tied to their hands, which were tied behind their heads. The slightest movements made the bridle tear the corners of their mouths. Some prisoners were thrown into a pit called the Hole, where they received only a cup of water and a slice of bread a day.

As a result, prisoners suffered severe psychological damage and some went insane. Others failed to rehabilitate themselves. Charles Dickens visited the prison and was horrified at what he saw. He vowed to expose the abuses. He was not alone in condemnation. When the abuses were publicized, public outrage forced reforms over a period of time. By the 1920s, the Quaker approach was abandoned.

Eastern State still had plenty of colorful history ahead of it before it finally closed down in 1971. In 1924, Pennsylvania Governor Gifford Pinchot's dog, Pep, became an inmate, complete with mugshot and prisoner number, C 2559. The story goes that Pinchot sent his dog to jail for life murdering his wife's cat. Most likely, this is a tall tale. According to the press, Pinchot donated Pep to the prison in order to raise the sorry state of morale.

Al Capone was one of numerous famous criminals imprisoned at Eastern State. He spent eight months there in 1929 and 1930. His cell was more like a luxury hotel room with his favorite pieces of furniture, including a radio and paintings. Capone lived in high style there, taking visitors, drinking whiskey, and smoking cigars.

Every prison has its escape artists, and Eastern State is no exception. In 1945, inmate Charles Klinedinst orchestrated a clever breakout for himself, Willie "Slick Willie" Sutton, and ten other men. Klinedinst was a plasterer by trade, and he masterminded the creation of a secret tunnel. For Klinedinst, freedom was short-lived. Two hours after his escape, he was captured and slammed back into his cell—with another ten years tacked on to his sentence. Sutton and the others were captured as well.

The facility was designated a historic site by the City of Philadelphia in 1958, and became a federal National Historic Landmark in 1965. Despite these merits, the prison was allowed to deteriorate. In 1971 it was shut down and prisoners were transferred to other institutions. The city considered tearing it down, but in the late 1980s a preservation movement began, and tours were initiated to raise funds. Eastern State officially became a historic tourist attraction in 1994, with tours, night-time ghosthunting, and a museum.

Visitors hoping to get spooked at Eastern State report a variety of ghostly sounds: muffled and intermingling voices, angry shouting, crying, wailing, footsteps, and clangs of heavy cell doors closing. Some of the sounds of voices are thought to be the phantom emotions of early prisoners forbidden to use their vocal chords. Every petal or spoke of cells has activity in it. Investigators have good odds of capturing EVP almost anywhere in the facility. Many of the cells are open, and on investigations you can sit inside them.

At Al Capone's fancy digs, people have captured or heard the sounds of a radio playing and voices talking. Capone was haunted himself while serving his time there—not by the ghosts of prisoners past, but by the ghost of a man he had murdered in the St. Valentine's Day massacre in Chicago in 1929, a bloody crime still fresh at the time Capone landed in Eastern State. Capone claimed that the ghostly James Clark followed him everywhere, threatening him. At Eastern State, Capone could be heard begging Jimmy to leave him alone. It did no good. Clark pestered Capone to his dying day—and perhaps beyond.

On one of my investigations at Eastern State, I was working with a colleague in Cellblock 4, using digital recorders and K2 meters. We stopped in front of different cells and posed questions, hoping to capture responses. At one, the lights on the meters flashed vigorously when we asked if someone was present who wished to communicate. For about half an hour, we talked to a communicator who identified herself as the sister of an inmate named Charles, who was serving time for robbery in the late nineteenth century. She seemed to think he was still there. Was she an earthbound soul? Perhaps—they are frequently encountered in haunted places. The communicator never gave any last names, making identities difficult to verify through records.

Cellblock 12, where violent criminals were housed, has some of the most spectacular activity. It has a heavy, brooding atmosphere. Dark, shadowy apparitions are seen. It is possible to access the upper level of the cellblock, and walk the narrow aisles next to cells and stand on catwalks to gaze down the length of the block.

On another occasion during one of my investigations, I went to Cellblock 12 with a small group of investigators literally in the middle of the night, around 3:00 A.M. We were clustered on the catwalk when we noticed shadows moving back and forth across the far end of the block. The shadows blocked faint light coming through a window. We started taking photographs and spreading out along the sides. It seemed that the more attention we paid the shadows, the more active they became. Some of us could see and feel them moving rapidly along the aisles behind us, creating cold breezes. Were they the ghosts of inmates and/or guards? No one knows, but it was a spectacular display.

On subsequent visits, I returned to Cellblock 12 in anticipation of the same, but—as is characteristic of the paranormal—got no exact repeats. I did, however, see shadowy forms again, but they did not behave at the same intensity.

Death Row is another area at Eastern State where people report good EVP. It's small and set apart from the spokes of cells.

Shadow figures are reported in other locations throughout the prison. In a characteristic encounter, a person starts to feel uneasy and watched, and then sees the dark silhouette of what appears to be a man. The figure remains still, as though it is watching the witness. But if the witness approaches it, the shadow darts away or vanishes.

The ghost of a man in the guard tower is frequently reported—perhaps the lasting imprint of one of the guards who had the alternately tense and boring job of watching over the prison yards.

Phantom cats are seen, usually outside the cellblocks and within the fortress walls. After the prison closed in 1971, a colony of feral cats took up residence there. They were fed by a man named Dan McCloud, who became known as "Dan the Cat Man." For twenty-eight years, McCloud visited the grounds and cared for the cats. Eventually they were neutered, and the colony decreased.

If you think you see a ghostly cat at night, just make sure it's not one of the thirty-nine white plaster statues set around the grounds, an art project memorializing the cats.

Photographs at Eastern State must be examined with care. The place has a lot of dust in it, and thus "orbs" show up easily.

There are different ways to experience Eastern State. A variety of tours are offered daily and seasonally. The prison also organizes its own after-hours tours at night. Or, you can sign up for a special private night-time ghost investigation arranged by a paranormal group renting the facility. The prison does not book these private events for you—you must locate them yourself. You may be able to learn of upcoming private events by surfing the Internet.

Spotlight on Ghosts
The Hexenkopf: Misery Mountain

Near Easton in Lehigh Valley sits a foreboding chunk of rock known as the Hexenkopf, a German term for "witch's head." Seen from certain angles, the hill resembles the head and face of a hag. Locals have called it Misery Mountain because of its history of bad luck, accidents, suicides, murders, mysterious fires, crop failures, and mishaps that happen in the vicinity, even into present times.

The one-thousand-foot-high Hexenkopf acquired its dark reputation in the eighteenth and nineteenth centuries when German immigrants, who became known as the Pennsylvania Dutch (a corruption of *Deutsch*), settled in the region. They brought with them from their homeland their superstitions and folklore about witches, ghosts, magic, spirits, and spells. It was whispered that when the mountain glowed at night, witches were holding their nocturnal revelries with the devil there. The glow may, in fact, have a natural explanation—the rock has a high mica content, which glints in the right conditions of moonlight.

The Hexenkopf is home to numerous ghosts and hauntings. The ghosts of witches and of the dead who died mysteriously or tragically on or near the hill have been seen and heard. On dark and windy nights, a headless man and a headless dog are seen in the area. Fiery, rolling balls of spectral fumes are supposedly the ghosts of two farmers who fought bitterly over property rights. Also seen is the ghost of a peg-legged farmer named Brown who reportedly fell to his death while chasing a witch. On moonless nights, he runs up behind people, making a stumping noise with his peg leg. He has gray hair and a beard, and a terrifying face.

A vanishing cart or car is a prominent feature in Hexenkopf lore. People travel up the steep hill never to come down the other side. One of the old stories tells of an abusive, violent man who mistreated his family and animals. One night he stormed off in a fit of anger to go to a tavern. He hitched up his horse-drawn wagon and mercilessly beat the horses all the way up the hill, giving them no rest. At the summit, a mist descended around man and animals, and they were never seen again.

The hill is also famous for its poisonous wind, which demons and witches blew off the mountain onto people and animals below. The wind sickened the living.

Mysterious, charmed animals have roamed the Hexenkopf for centuries. In the eighteenth century, a charmed white fox was seen one winter. As long as it was about, hunters could kill no game. They could not kill the fox, either, not even by poison bait. Shots fired at it missed. Local people believed that the fox was the embodiment of all the evil spirits who resided on the hill.

CHAPTER 5

Fort Mifflin
PHILADELPHIA

BATTLEFIELDS AND FORTS all have their resident ghosts, but Fort Mifflin ranks high on the list when it comes to the paranormal. Visitors and investigators say it is one of the most haunted places in the country. Come here especially on a moonlit night, and you will be certain to agree! The fort's most famous ghosts are the Screaming Lady and the Faceless Man, and there are plenty of other phantom activities to tingle your spine. Apparitions are reported moving about the open areas of the fort, and many of the buildings and casements are hot spots of activity.

The fourteen buildings of the fort sit on fifty acres on Mud Island, a stone's throw from Philadelphia and the Philadelphia

International Airport. In fact, the fort is directly beneath the landing pattern for the airport.

Fort Mifflin has a brave but checkered history. It was originally intended as a stone-walled British fort to guard the colonial empire. Construction began in 1771, but was halted within a year because the British were sensing the rising revolutionary sentiments. When the Revolutionary War began in earnest in 1776, defenses were organized for Philadelphia and its port at the mouth of the Delaware River. The rebels built Fort Mercer on the New Jersey side, and completed Fort Mifflin on the Pennsylvania side of the river. Mifflin was finished mostly in wood and earth instead of stone as originally planned by the British. It took its name from Major General Thomas Mifflin, who supervised the construction, and who later became the first governor of Pennsylvania.

In the fall of 1777, the British made an intensive assault on both forts. General William Howe, Commander-in-Chief of the British Army, had earlier defeated George Washington's troops at the battles of Brandywine and Germantown. His army was badly in need of supplies, which were held on British ships in the Delaware River. The British held the city of Philadelphia, but the Continental Army held the surrounding areas, including access via the Delaware River. Howe had to break past the rebels in order to get the supplies off the ships.

Howe and his Hessian allies bombarded the forts. Fort Mifflin was destroyed and rebuilt as the colonial rebels stood fast. But the British soon prevailed after weeks of heavy shelling. More than ten thousand cannonballs were blasted at the fort from three sides. Grapeshot, which shredded flesh, took a heavy toll as well. It was the largest bombardment of the entire Revolutionary War.

Washington was well aware of the strategic value of the fort and stated on November 5, "Fort Mifflin is of the utmost importance to our cause and must be saved at all costs."

On November 15, British and Hessian forces used a back channel to overrun the fort and set it afire. Casualties ran about 70 percent, and the remaining survivors fled into the night. The delay caused to the British enabled General George Washington to get his troops to Valley Forge, where they recuperated for the winter. Had he not been able to do so, the outcome of the war might have been much different.

Fort Mifflin was not rebuilt again until after the war was over, in 1798. More buildings were added up to 1875, including the bomb-proof casements and the stone perimeter wall. The fort saw action in the War of 1812. During the Civil War, Confederate soldiers were jailed there. In the twentieth century, ammunition and supplies were kept at the fort during World Wars I and II, and the Korean War. In 1954, the fort was decommissioned and became a nonprofit historical site. It went nearly to ruins and then was restored to its 1834 appearance.

The present buildings include an officers' quarters, enlisted barracks, a blacksmith shop, casements, powder magazine, arsenal (originally a prison), and batteries (now minus most of the guns).

The fort is open to tourists during the day and has sponsored all-night ghosthunting events, including sleepovers featuring noted demonologist and paranormal investigator John Zaffis. It has also opened its grounds to groups for private investigations.

I investigated at Fort Mifflin with members of the Center for Paranormal Studies and Investigation. We were given an extensive tour and history of the place by Lorraine Irby, the office manager who looks after the site with her husband, Wayne.

The Screaming Woman is encountered in the officers' quarters. Her identity is debated and the original legend about her has been debunked. The prevailing story holds that she is Elizabeth Pratt, who was married to an officer and lived in the officers' quarters. Her daughter wanted to marry an enlisted man, and her parents opposed the match. The distraught daughter contracted typhoid fever and died. Elizabeth screamed and screamed in grief and hanged herself. So vivid and loud are the screams that on occasion the Philadelphia police have been called.

The real Elizabeth was married to a sergeant, not an officer, and would not have lived in the officers' quarters. Instead, she and her husband lived in a shack in the back of the fort. Elizabeth died in 1803, along with her infant daughter, of typhoid fever.

So who is the Screaming Woman? No one knows, but scream she does. Lorraine heard the screaming one night. She was asleep, but awakened by a horrible scream. Her first thought was that one of the nocturnal ghosthunting visitors was in trouble. She ran outside and saw two visitors sitting on the porch of the officer's quarters, talking as though nothing had happened. "Did you hear that scream?" she asked them. They shook their heads—they had not heard a thing. "What I heard sounded like a younger woman in her twenties," Lorraine told us. Other employees have heard the same sounds.

On one investigation, John Zaffis was in Elizabeth's room with one other person. Around three or four in the morning, they suddenly heard the sounds of a man and woman arguing. The voices were muffled and words could not be distinguished. "The voices went back and forth for about five minutes," Zaffis said. "At the same time, we smelled a heavy scent of perfume mixed with talcum powder. It reminded me of something a grandmother would wear."

Lorraine has smelled the strong scent of talcum in the officer's quarters. Once she was upstairs with Zaffis and other investigators. They went into the back room, where much of the paranormal activity has been reported. She saw a shadowy figure in the room. She has felt a deep chill in the same area.

At Halloween, costumed re-enactors stage dramas for entertainment. One year, the actresses playing Elizabeth and her daughter were sitting at a table in the officers' quarters when the glass globe of one of the oil lamps detached itself and rolled off. It did not break. "They would not come in here the rest of the night," Lorraine said. EVP have been recorded in the quarters, including a male voice that orders, "Get out!"

The Faceless Man appears in Casement 5. He is thought to be the ghost of Billy Howe, a Civil War prisoner who was the only person ever executed by hanging at the fort. Billy was a deserter who was convicted of murder. He escaped and was captured. A year after his execution, he was exonerated.

Billy is seen sewing in the casement, a black hole where his facial features should be. A tall male form, about six feet two inches, dressed in a sloppy coat, has been photographed in Casement 5 by at least two persons. In both photos, the figure has no face. The Faceless Man seems mean and mocking, according to visitors.

All of the casements have activity, including apparitions and murmuring voices, believed to be the remnants of other Civil War prisoners. In 2006, Wayne Irby was mowing grass when he noticed a depression in the ground. It turned out to be the location of an unknown casement, hidden for more than 130 years. The Irbys contacted Zaffis to have it checked out. Zaffis and his team were the first to enter the haunted Casement 11, on September 16 of that year. Billy Howe was held here after his capture until his execution.

"There was a lot of energy in the casement," said Zaffis, recalling the event. "It was really something—it took us right back into the past."

Many people record EVPs in Casement 11 and also feel presences.

Casement 1 once held two hundred Confederate prisoners in extremely camped conditions. EVP have captured a man's voice identifying himself as "Michael." Michael seems friendly and likes the visitors who come to the fort. Witnesses have seen one of the bunks move by itself.

In Casement 4, a presence makes attacks on blonde women. Victims feel pinched and grabbed and experience unpleasant sensations.

In the blacksmith's shop, the ghost of Jacob the blacksmith has been seen. He preferred the back door of his shop to be left open, which was not allowed. There have been problems with the door remaining shut ever since—even when it was locked. Finally the door was removed because the constant opening was breaking the hinges. People have reported seeing the tools move slightly as if on their own.

In the powder magazine, some people have sensed a negative presence, and they feel watched. A strange mist has been photographed here, and shadowy forms have been seen moving about. The silhouette of a soldier has been seen in the doorway, as though someone is still standing guard. EVP recordings have captured odd sounds, like anvils clanging together.

In the artillery shed, the voice of a ghostly little girl calls out for help.

The southwest sally port is near the back channel where General Howe found the Achilles heel of the fort and finally broke its defenses. The area has a heavy feel to it that affects some people physically. People have felt touched or poked by invisible hands. Some people feel so uneasy they cannot stay long in the spot.

Near the commandant's house, the voice of a little girl cries out "Mommy" in a long wail. She is believed to be the victim of the typhoid fever epidemic in the early eighteenth century.

If you see a tour guide dressed in a Revolutionary War uniform, look twice. He's not a re-enactor, but a ghost, and he is said to give a very good tour. His apparition has been spotted most often at the powder magazine.

Another frequently seen specter is the lamplighter, who appears around the enlisted men's barracks. It was customary in earlier times for a lamplighter to light the oil lamps at the fort.

One obstacle at Fort Mifflin is the constant roar of jets over-head as planes land at the busy Philadelphia airport. They are near touchdown as they fly over the fort, so they are low and loud. The noise can interfere with EVP, and with the ability to hear some of the subtler phantom sounds. Even with the jet noise, however, Fort Mifflin is a phantom paradise, well worth the visit.

If you spend an evening or a night at the fort, take the elements into consideration. Much of your time will be spent outdoors. Take plenty of layered clothing and a flashlight. Mosquitoes are ferocious in the summer.

CHAPTER 6

Riegelsville Inn
RIEGELSVILLE

RIEGELSVILLE IS ONE OF THOSE sleepy little Bucks County towns that exudes mystery. If it isn't haunted, it looks like it should be. And haunted it is. For such a small place, ghosts abound.

Riegelsville sits on the Delaware River, which is wide and serene in this region. Part of the town is in Pennsylvania and part of it lies across a quaint bridge in New Jersey. A paper mill was once the dominant industry here. In fact, the town is named after its founders, the Benjamin Riegel family, the owners of the Riegel Paper Corporation. Today the town thrives on antiques and tourism. A lot of "city folk" from Manhattan and Philadelphia—both only an hour away—like to retreat to country homes here on weekends and during the summer.

Highway 611 winds along the Pennsylvania side of the Delaware, and the drive is a beautiful excursion through lush terrain, especially in the summer. It evokes lazy days, fishing, boating, and sitting out on porches with a glass of cold lemonade. In winter, the little town inns and pubs beckon like havens warmed by glowing hearth fires and hearty meals.

If you approach Riegelsville from the New Jersey side, you go across the quaint Roebling Bridge, and the Riegelsville Inn is the first building you see—an impressive sight. From the Pennsylvania side, you get off the highway, wind a short way through town, cross the towpath, and suddenly the inn looms ahead of you. Either way you travel, the Riegelsville Inn will pull you in, even if you hadn't planned on stopping in town. The three-story white stone inn has an inviting veranda and an enclosed second-floor porch where guests can enjoy the country atmosphere, the spectacular river, and the occasional car and cyclist on the bridge. They may even be treated to one of the several ghosts residing inside.

Riegelsville Inn was built by founding father Benjamin Riegel as a place for travelers and townsfolk. In 1838, Riegel bought a piece of land and built the inn. Over the years, thousands of guests spent time here. A few seem to have stayed on as ghosts.

The inn was closed for a few years in the 1990s. After a change in ownership, it was renovated and reopened. The ambience was preserved, and diners and overnight guests can still enjoy a nineteenth-century feel and lots of well-oiled, richly glowing wood. There are three dining rooms, a comfortable pub, and eight guest rooms upstairs.

The most active haunted areas have been in the kitchen, the men's restroom, and the second floor where there are two guest rooms. People who have stayed in Room 10 have had ghostly experiences. Diners also have seen phantoms.

On the day of my visit, the pub was tended by a young woman named Emily, who had worked at the inn for twelve years. Having grown up in a haunted house in Riegelsville, Emily was accustomed to unusual phenomena. Some of the guests and other staff members have not been so calm, however.

"Things get misplaced and moved around," Emily said. "Most of it seems to be done by the ghosts of two little boys and a little girl. There is a story that a little girl was violently killed on the porch and was dragged to the river."

Like a lot of ghosts, especially child ghosts, there is rarely historical corroboration to verify the legends. True or not, the ghosts are more than real to multiple witnesses. Several stories of little girl ghosts revolve around the inn.

Once a customer came in to the pub with a friend and his two children. He went upstairs to the men's room, and when he came back down he grabbed Emily's arm. "You know this place is haunted," he said in an urgent voice.

Emily was busy making drink orders and nodded matter-of-factly, saying, "Yes, I know." "No, this place is *really* haunted," the man insisted. "I just talked to one of the ghosts!"

He then related that a little girl had followed him into the men's room and said, "Why doesn't anyone talk to me? Everybody ignores me and walks past me." Suddenly, the man realized he was talking with a ghost, and he left the men's room in a hurry.

Another story is told that a male guest walked up the stairs to the third floor, where he found a little girl sitting on the floor hugging her knees to her chest. "Why are you here?" asked the man. To his astonishment, the little girl vanished.

The ghost of a little girl also once followed housekeepers around. The maids would find linens mysteriously torn off freshly made beds.

Meanwhile, a prankster ghost has enjoyed overturning the coffee pot filter in the kitchen.

Once three of us were closing down," said Emily. "There were no guests. We heard a big slam in the kitchen. We found the coffee filter had somehow come out of the coffee pot and flown across the room and landed upside down on the floor. That happened several times. We never saw it happen. We always heard the noise and then found the filter on the floor."

A portrait of Christopher Columbus continually fell off its wall hook for a period of time. The picture would fall when no one was looking; it would be found with its glass broken. It would be repaired and rehung, only to fall and break again. Finally, the picture was retired. Several employees were happy—they had never liked the image of Columbus, whose eyes seemed to follow people when they walked past.

An employee lived in Room 10 for a period of time. She reported a strange orb of light that appeared frequently in the room; her young daughter talked to someone who was invisible. The black silhouette of a person standing at the foot of the bed in that room has startled some guests in the middle of the night.

In the downstairs dining and bar areas, the apparition of a woman wearing a long gray skirt walks about, her skirt making swishing sounds as she goes.

The ghosts apparently did not appreciate some repainting and rearranging of furniture done by the chef. During the repainting of one of the dining rooms, the staff came in one morning and found that all of the bread plates that had been put on the dining tables the night before were all stacked in the kitchen. At least they were not broken!

Some employees have heard their names called out by unknown voices and have heard strange knocking sounds on the walls.

Spotlight on Ghosts: Washington's Bogus Vision

A persistent piece of folklore involving George Washington concerns an elaborate vision he supposedly had in the winter of 1777 while stationed with his troops at Valley Forge, Pennsylvania. It is a soaring, flag-waving story—but a complete piece of fiction. Nonetheless, it proliferates as a bit of actual history.

The story goes that one day Washington sat alone for a long time in his office. He had a vision of the destiny of the United States, heralded by a trumpeting angel. The vision foretold the victorious outcome of the Revolutionary War, and then the outcome of the Civil War, and finally a "red" threat from overseas interpreted in modern times as Communism and World War III. The angel told Washington that America would face three great perils. Washington supposedly confided this vision to a man named Anthony Sherman.

I went to Valley Forge to try to document this experience, and I spoke with a historian there. I learned that no such experience was ever recorded in any of Washington's letters or diaries. Nor was there a record of any man named Anthony Sherman. Furthermore, the historian said it is unlikely that Washington would have had more than a moment to himself in his quarters at Valley Forge, which teemed with activity and constant demands upon his attention. And if he had experienced such a remarkable vision, he surely would have told someone of importance, not a lowly soldier.

The story of the vision was first published in a magazine in 1880. The article's author, Wesley Bradshaw, claimed to have heard it from Sherman on July 4, 1859, when he was ninety-nine years old. Supposedly the old man was the only person in whom Washington ever confided the vision.

The tale seems to have been concocted to inspire patriotism. It continues to be used in that way today. It's colorful fiction—but not fact.

CENTRAL PENNSYLVANIA

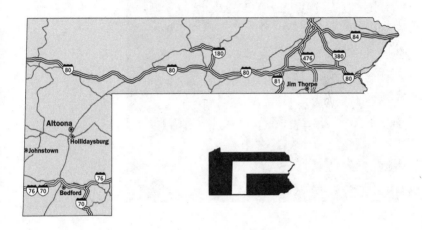

Altoona
   Baker Mansion

Bedford
   Jean Bonnet Tavern

Hollidaysburg
   U.S. Hotel

Jim Thorpe
   The Inn at Jim Thorpe
   The Old Jail Museum

Johnstown
   Greater Johnstown/
   Cambria County Convention and
   Visitors Bureau

CHAPTER 7

Baker Mansion
ALTOONA

THE SHOWPIECE HOME of Elias Baker, a Victorian-era iron master, boasts a collection of ghosts along with the historical furniture and objects. The mansion can be seen only on a guided tour, and sometimes the ghosts tag along.

Elias Baker was a man with big ambitions. Living with his family in Lancaster, he saw a good business opportunity in the growing iron industry in Blair County. In 1836, he and a cousin purchased the Allegheny Furnace in central Pennsylvania, which had been built in 1811. He loaded up his worldly goods, wife Hetty and sons Woods and Sylvester into a horse-drawn wagon and moved west. They settled into a simple, small home near the furnace. Baker applied himself to building a fortune by smelting iron ore. The couple had a daughter, Anna, followed in three years by another girl, Margaretta, who died of diphtheria when she was two.

Baker's furnace prospered and he soon bought out his cousin. He employed about fifty workers, and paid them in scrip, which could be redeemed only at his goods store. What a deal! Real money came quickly to Baker, thanks to the flourishing iron trade. Within a few years, he wanted to show off his new wealth with a fancy home. It was the custom of the time for the rich, especially the newly rich, to advertise their success in a showy home that shouted money. Baker was no exception.

In 1845, Baker commissioned a twenty-eight-room Greek revival mansion in Altoona. Everything about it and in it had to have class and be in impeccably good taste. After he committed to building the home, Baker was caught by falling iron prices. He would not cut back on the extravagance he planned and pressed ahead. The mansion cost fifteen thousand dollars and was completed in 1849. Marble fireplaces were imported from Italy, along with hand-carved oak furniture from Belgium. The house was filled with fancy plaster work, black walnut woodwork, and the latest features, such as central heating, speaking tubes connecting the different floors (for the Bakers to summon servants), and a dumb waiter. There was no indoor plumbing or electricity. By modern standards, the home seems austere, but in its day it was a statement of success and wealth.

Baker used a great deal of iron in his new home: the railings on the side porch, the window sills, and the bases and capitals of the massive Greek columns. He originally wanted to make the columns entirely of iron, but they proved to be too heavy, and he had to use cement instead. The iron was painted to look like stone, and sand was thrown on the wet paint to give it a rough finish. The exterior walls were originally faced in lead, which was replaced with limestone.

His son Woods (full name David Woods) was not interested in the iron business and moved to Philadelphia in adulthood. He married Sarah Tuthill and they had one daughter, Louisa. Tragically, at age twenty-eight, Woods was killed in a steamboat accident. His baby daughter was only two-and-a-half weeks old.

Elias Baker enjoyed his splendid home until his death in 1864. The business was taken over by his son Sylvester, who managed it for twenty years. Sylvester, Hetty, and Anna, who never married, continued to live in the mansion. Hetty died in 1900 at age ninety-six, and Sylvester, who also never married, died in 1907. He expired in one of the family sitting rooms. He lay down on the sofa to take a nap. When he got up, he collapsed and died, probably of a heart attack or stroke. Anna died in 1914, and the mansion was closed.

In 1922, the Blair County Historical Society took over the mansion and opened it as a museum. It is a favorite tourist destination today. Visitors are impressed by its Southern-looking grandeur and by its fine collection of furnishings. In addition to the Baker possessions, the home has donations of furnishings that fit the era.

There are numerous stories of ghostly activities at the mansion. Some of them have been debunked, but many experiences remain unexplained. The tour of the mansion lasts one-and-a-half hours. The tour covers plenty of detail, including the ghostly activity, if you ask.

The day I visited the mansion, I was fortunate enough to have a one-on-one guided tour. My guide told me she was skeptical of ghosts and had had no unusual experiences herself in the three years she had been there, but she acknowledged that others had.

One of the favorite ghostly tales concerns a wedding dress that used to be on display in a glass case on the second floor.

The dress belonged to Sarah Dyster, who supposedly stole one of Anna's boyfriends. Anna was jealous of Sarah's wedding. Another story goes that Anna fell in love with one of her father's laborers and was forbidden to marry him. She vowed she would never marry and was jealous of Sarah when she wed. Her ghost shakes the dress in anger.

It's a romance tragedy tale, but there's no truth to it, I learned. The Bakers were class conscious, and it is unlikely that Anna would have ever mingled with the "common" people, let alone gotten romantically involved with them. Whether or not she ever visited the furnace is unknown. In fact, she had some chances to marry men of her station, but the relationships did not progress.

As for the shaking, there is an explanation. It was discovered that pressing down on certain floorboards caused the glass case to wiggle slightly, making it look as though the dress was shaking or "dancing."

The wedding dress is no longer on display, which has fueled rumors that it was taken down because it was haunted. According to Wright, the dress had stood in the case for thirty years, much longer than recommended for the preservation of the fabric. The material was deteriorating. The dress was placed in storage, awaiting the funds for restoration.

Dress or no, the ghost of Anna is reportedly seen in her bedroom on the second floor. She also may be a ghost spotted walking around the grounds. A few years ago, a woman who was playing tennis in the park across the street from the mansion observed a woman dressed in period clothes come out of the house, walk down the driveway, and watch her. She thought there might be a tour going on, and the woman was one of the guides. When the woman was done playing tennis, the mysterious figure walked back up the drive and vanished.

There are plenty other unexplained phenomena, too. The

ghost of Elias Baker has been seen walking about his beloved home. Visitors experience sudden and intense cold spots.

A little boy ghost has been seen in the home and also looking out a window. No one knows who he is, as no male children were born in the house. Wright told me the windows are always kept shuttered.

Bonnie K. has worked at the mansion since 1980 and told me she has had numerous ghostly or unexplained experiences. When she first started, she was alone in the mansion until about noon. Now there is an office upstairs, and others come to work in the mornings. However, Bonnie still spends time alone in the house as she cleans.

"I'm not afraid here," she said of her experiences, noting that the ghosts are friendly. She has seen lights turn on and off inexplicably in different rooms.

On one occasion, Bonnie was cleaning the crystal chandelier that hangs in the dining room. The chandelier was not owned by the Bakers, but was added to the house later.

"I was standing on a ladder taking the prisms down," said Bonnie. "There were three people in front of me and no one behind me. One lady had her dog with her. I made the remark, 'I don't care how many servants the Bakers had, I bet I keep this house cleaner than they do.' Just then, something whacked me across the back of the legs and the dog took after something over to the door."

Apparently the ghosts eavesdrop!

"Another time I was in the bathroom downstairs in the basement, washing my hands," Bonnie said. "I could feel a hand touching the back of my neck going up over my head. At first I thought it was a bat and I jerked down, but there was nothing there. But I could feel that hand like anything."

Bonnie thinks she heard the ghost of Sylvester walking about. In his later years, Sylvester walked with a cane, and made a stumping sound as we went along. "I was here totally by myself," Bonnie said. "When I went downstairs to the lower level, I felt the presence of someone. I wasn't scared. I was working along, and then I heard somebody walking as though with a cane, thump-thump-thump, and then it was out the door and was gone."

Bonnie also saw what may have been a ghost dressed in period clothes. "There was a group of us waiting for the mansion to open," she said. "We were all standing on the porch. The curator came. When he opened, I turned around and there was a man behind me who was dressed in the period clothes that the Bakers would have worn. I didn't think anything of it, because sometimes people do come here in costume and take pictures or whatever. As everyone got their things and were leaving, they said, 'Now you'll be here by yourself.' I said, 'What about the gentleman who came in behind me?' Nobody knew who I was talking about!"

Spotlight on Ghosts: The Phantom Hitchhiker of Wopsy Lookout

The phantom hitchhiker is one of the most common types of ghosts. They are found everywhere around the world and usually are lone female ghosts wandering roads looking for a ride home or to a particular destination. According to lore, they look and act so real that the living are fooled, and offer them a lift. They disappear at their destination or vanish from the back seat of a car. The stories of their tragedies are seldom verifiable by history and fact, but they seize hold in popular lore and take on a weird reality all their own.

In Pennsylvania, one of the most famous phantom hitchhikers is an unnamed woman dressed in white who wanders Wopsononock Mountain (known as Wopsy Lookout) near Altoona. She is searching in vain for her dead husband who died with her in an accident.

Wopsy Lookout sports an impressive view, which has drawn many visitors through the years. A hotel once stood at the top, but it burned down long ago. The Juniata Gap Road (formerly Beulah Road) that leads to the top of the mountain is treacherous, especially at a curve called the Devil's Elbow, where many accidents have occurred.

The story goes that the young woman and man were on their honeymoon, riding up to the hotel. Their carriage went out of control at Devil's Elbow, plunging off the mountain, killing them both. The young husband's body was never recovered. The ghost of his wife, all in white, drifts up and down the road, endlessly looking for him. Sometimes she is said to carry a candle.

According to different versions of the story, she accosts young men in anger and examines them to see if they are her man.

Sometimes she hitches rides, usually with young men, and then she disappears as soon as the car gets to Devil's Elbow. One modern account tells of a man who picked her up and was startled that he could not see her in the rear-view mirror but could see her when he turned around and looked. She disappeared from his vehicle at Devil's Elbow.

The ghost is known as the White Lady of Wopsononock. She's also called the White Lady of the Buckhorn because she can be seen from the access to the lookout coming from Buckhorn Mountain on the opposite side.

The story of the white lady is similar to another famous hitchhiking ghost, Resurrection Mary of Chicago. That young phantom is said to have gone ballroom dancing one night but left on foot after an argument with her date. She walked along the highway and was struck by a car and killed. Her ghost usually asks for a ride "home," which is Resurrection Cemetery where she is allegedly buried.

Phantom hitchhikers never find what they are looking for. They are stuck in an eternal loop of repetition, much like the famous phantom Flying Dutchman who can never land his ship at port.

CHAPTER 8

The U.S. Hotel
HOLLIDAYSBURG

THE U.S. HOTEL IS NO LONGER A HOTEL—at least for people. A number of colorful ghosts have permanent residence there, and they are more than willing to entertain the patrons who come to the restaurant and bar for food and drink.

In the early days of the 1800s, Hollidaysburg boomed as part of the rapidly growing iron industry. The Juniata iron in the area was considered to be of exceptional quality and was in high demand. The Pennsylvania Canal, completed in 1832, was built along the Juniata River to serve the iron trade and hotels. Businesses sprang up like mushrooms along its banks. One of the best was the U.S. Hotel, built by John Dougherty. Beginning in 1835, the hotel offered food, drink, and lodging to the booming canal and river traffic.

The hotel has twenty-two rooms upstairs, and the interior is laid out like an "H".

Life was prosperous until November 29, 1871, when a fire destroyed much of the hotel. The catastrophe broke Dougherty's spirit, and he never rebuilt. Instead, he sold the ruins in 1886 to a German immigrant, Engelbert Gromiller, a brewmaster with big ambitions. Gromiller rebuilt the hotel, and it still stands today, a grand and comfortable Victorian establishment with old world charm.

Gromiller added a brewery and began producing fine German beer. It was a smart move, for the iron trade gave way to the steel industry, the canal shut down, and business changed. Railroad tracks were built in place of the canal. In 1905, Gromiller added a bar. Some of its original features, such as leaded stained glass windows, a hand-carved mahogany bar, a brass foot trail, and spittoon trough, are still there.

During World War II, the U.S. Navy used the building for a radio school and turned the bar into a shower room. The Navy also housed seriously wounded soldiers in the hotel, and some of them died in their beds. After the war, the hotel suffered the fate of many such establishments, going through changes of ownership and sinking into a gentle decline. The brewery was destroyed.

In 1994, the U.S. Hotel was purchased by Karen and Jason Yoder, who began an ongoing restoration program. The original bar and kitchen were turned into dining rooms.

The U.S. Hotel has three floors, but only the first floor, the dining rooms, and bar are open to the public. The old hotel rooms upstairs have some of the old furniture and beds in them, and some have been turned into storage areas.

The hotel's ghosts drift around on all levels, however. "People have seen different apparitions," said Kim Yoder, daughter-in-law of the owners, who works at the establishment. "There is a man with a tall Abraham Lincoln-style hat who sits in a booth in Dining Room 1. A female ghost likes to brush people in the dining rooms."

"The lady," as the ghost is called, especially haunts the back dining room called "the parlor." Some diners have glimpsed her whitish form.

"One customer told me that on her first visit to the hotel, she walked in with her husband and saw the apparition of the lady," Yoder said. "She was wearing a dress and floating through the hallway. Her husband did not see it."

On her second visit, the woman, who was a medium, came by herself and sat in a booth. She asked Yoder, "Do you work here early in the morning?"

"Yes, I do," answered Yoder.

"The ghosts want you to know that they are comfortable with you and are watching out for you."

The information was reassuring. Although Yoder has never been frightened by anything and considers the ghosts friendly, some of their escapades and appearances have been unsettling.

"When I first started working here, I was a nonbeliever," said Yoder. "But there have been things that are unexplainable. I tend to be more of a believer now."

It is usually Yoder's job to open up between six and seven o'clock in the morning. She is the only person in the hotel at that time. Her routine is to open the hall door, turn on the lamp on the hostess station, unlock the front door, and check the dining rooms, among other tasks. The lamp is a banker's lamp with a rectangular green glass shade.

"One day I came in and the desk lamp shade was flipped all the way up," said Yoder. "I flipped it back down. I unlocked the front door and walked through each dining room. When I came back around to the hostess station, the desk lamp shade was flipped back up." Yoder felt a bit unnerved. "I quickly went to my office and just stayed there," she said.

Another unexplained incident took place early in the morning. " I was sitting in my office. There was no one in the building. There is a candy machine by the bar. I heard the sounds of someone getting candy. I could hear the clear sound of the candy falling. I poked my head around the corner but there was no one there. I sat back down at my desk. Half an hour later, it happened again!" Whoever had the sweet tooth remains unknown.

Strange things happen at late hours, too. Bartenders closing up by themselves turn off the television. The next morning, the TV is on and set to a channel showing only static.

"Recently I closed the bar—the first time I ever closed the bar by myself," said Yoder. "There were a few people in here after last call. It was about 2:30 in the morning. They were friends of mine and were getting ready to leave. One of them is a large guy, over six feet tall, kind of husky, one who is not going to be afraid of anything. He was walking out the door when he suddenly screamed. He said he felt someone invisible touch his arm. We all got the chills. I said, 'I have to close this place by myself. Can you make sure I get out okay?'"

While Yoder was talking to her friends, she heard three loud knocks. "They sounded like they came from inside the building. No one commented on it. I heard it again. I said, "Did anyone hear that?"" Everyone said they did. But none of us knew where they came from."

A little boy ghost likes to play with things—perhaps he is the one who moves objects, turns lights on and off, and makes strange noises. Customers have seen him sitting on the steps outside the main door.

Other odd phenomena include small balls of light that zip

through the dining rooms, a locked cabinet that is found mysteriously open without explanation, silverware that flies off the tables, and glasses on kitchen shelves that topple and break. Customers have seen the lights in the hallway swing by themselves.

The upper floors are off-limits to customers, but can be accessed on certain ghost investigations, tours, and events. Al Brinzda, the founder of the Allegheny Mountain Ghosthunters, has been researching and investigating at the hotel since 2000 both day and night. He gave me a tour of the upstairs, and we spent several hours investigating with equipment.

What can you expect if you gain access to floors two and three? Brinzda, who is psychically sensitive, has encountered a wide range of phenomena. He has been pushed off balance by a force that moved past him He captured digital photographs of a dark shadowy figure in the hallway on the second floor, and others have seen what may be the same dark figure on other occasions. In the same hallway, the ghost of a World War II soldier is seen, as though he is standing guard.

The ghost of a man hanging by the neck from pipes has been seen in Bedroom 1. He is thought to have committed suicide, but such a death has not yet been historically documented. Brinzda has gotten EVP here of a man saying "Frank" and a boy with a British accent saying "ectoplasm."

Brinzda said that a painter working in the hotel once stayed overnight in Bedroom 2. In the morning, he was startled to see the ghost of a woman in the hallway. Or at least half a woman. She was visible only from the waist up, and appeared to be wearing a white dress with a high collar. She floated along the hallway. The painter left and never stayed overnight again.

Brindza has seen the ghost of a young woman sitting on one of the beds, looking as though she is wounded with gashes on her body. He tuned in psychically to the spirit of a man who said he had been beaten and stabbed to death in the hotel.

In Room 10, a woman died. The ghost of a little boy—perhaps the same one seen elsewhere in the hotel—has been seen in and near the room.

The AMG team has seen lights hanging from the ceiling swing inexplicably.

Orbs that seem to have intelligence and move about are seen on many occasions.

One of the more intriguing ghosts is called Stinky, because he appears as a scrawny, dirty man with long greasy hair and rotting teeth. He has given the name "Spiro" in EVP. Stinky is never in a good mood. He prefers to haunt a back bedroom on the third floor, Room 12, which has been dubbed "Stinky's Room." He once told a female investigator in EVP, "I'll be your worst nightmare." Fortunately, Stinky stays upstairs and does not bother restaurant and bar patrons.

Spotlight on Ghosts: Ectoplasmic Ghosts?

Many haunted locations have albums of photographs taken on premises by visitors. Some of them show cloudy mists that weave around the objects in the photos. The mists may look like fog or smog, or uneven layers and streams of smoke. Ghost enthusiasts call this phenomenon ectoplasm or "ecto" for short. When it shows up in a photograph, they say, it reveals a ghost or spirit. Is ecto really paranormal or a case of mistaken identity?

Whether or not ectoplasm is a genuine substance, belief in it persists, perhaps due in part to the popularity of the 1982 film *Ghostbusters*. The origins of ectoplasm date to the nineteenth century when Spiritualism and séances were all the rage. The word was coined in 1894 by a French researcher, Charles Richet, who combined two Greek words, *ektos* and *plasma*, to mean "exteriorized substance." Richet used it to describe a weird third arm that oozed out of the noses, mouths, ears, and other body orifices of mediums during trance states. Supposedly, ectoplasm was used by spirits to materialize bodies in the physical world.

Ectoplasm was warm to the touch and smelly. It ranged in texture, such as dough, rubber, cotton, muslin, gauze, and froth. It would come out in shapeless masses, or form into ghostly hands and feet, as well as other parts of a spirit "body." Sometimes ectoplasm seemed more like a vapor or smoke.

From its beginnings, ectoplasm was controversial, and was uncovered as fraudulent in some cases. Sometimes the "ecto" turned out to be nothing more than soap, gelatin, and egg white. Researchers tested mediums by forcing them to drink blueberry juice or dyes, in case they had secreted cotton or linen in their stomachs to regurgitate. Other mediums performed séances in the nude to prove that they were not faking it. Research of ectoplasm ended for the most part by the mid-twentieth century with the jury out on whether or not it is a genuine spirit manifestation.

The latest twist of ecto has emerged in photography, especially images taken with digital cameras in haunted locations. Those white mists usually have a natural explanation; the camera has captured humid moisture in the air that is invisible to the human eye but is illuminated by a camera flash. Sometimes cigarette smoke is the culprit. Nearly invisible wisps of smoke can linger in the air long after a cigarette has been extinguished.

So, most ecto or ghost mist photos probably have natural explanations. Some photos, however, do defy explanation, keeping the debate going and the intrigue high.

CHAPTER 9

Jean Bonnet Tavern
BEDFORD

NESTLED IN THE ROLLING COUNTRYSIDE between Bedford and Schellsburg in Bedford County, the Jean Bonnet Tavern makes an ideal stop for those who want cozy colonial surroundings, hearty food, and maybe a ghost or two for entertainment. The hauntings are gentle here, including industrious, hard-working ghosts and ghosts who like to savor a meal and a drink. They'll give you plenty to talk about, but they won't deter you from coming back again and again to this enchanting establishment.

The tavern has a distinguished history stretching back to pre-Revolutionary War days. The land on which it was built was part of a 690-acre tract owned by the William Penn family. A land speculator, Hans Ireland, acquired the land, and in 1762 Ireland sold it to Robert Callender, an Indian trader. Callender, who later became a scout for General George Washington, had the stone and chestnut beam tavern built in the 1760s. The establishment was bought by Jean Bonnet and his wife in 1779, who ran it as a public house. Their name became the namesake of the tavern.

The building was typical for its day, made of fieldstone and oak timbers, with large fire places to put out a lot of heat, and low ceilings to retain the heat. They built them to last in those days, and last the Jean Bonnet has. Stepping inside is like traveling back in time to rustic colonial days. George Washington and his troops stayed here, and today the place probably doesn't look much different, save for the modernizations. As was typical in earlier times, taverns and inns did double duty as courthouses, and the Jean Bonnet was no exception. Trials took place here, and some of the condemned were hanged on the spot, inside the premises.

The Jean Bonnet has an early American dining room downstairs, and a casual tavern upstairs that boasts an impressive selection of microbrew and draft beer. There are only four guest rooms, all furnished in colonial decor. The present owners are Melissa and Tom Jacobs.

The tavern is home to a variety of ghosts who may be imprints of times long past, people who worked there, stayed there, and perhaps lived and died there.

According to one story about the Revolutionary War days, the ghost of a forlorn young woman haunts the place as she awaits her long-lost lover. During the war, her fiancé was a scout for Washington (not Callender, the early owner). They arranged to meet each other at the Jean Bonnet. The young woman arrived in eager anticipation of seeing her lover. He failed to come at the appointed time. She waited and waited, spending long periods gazing out the window, hoping to see him approach in the distance. Days passed, and weeks passed, and her anxiety grew. She clung to the hope that he was just delayed by the business of war, or had gotten stuck somewhere. The weeks became months, and she fell into sorrow and despair. Eventually, she became seriously ill and then died, reportedly of a broken heart. She never knew that her fiancé did not make their lovers' rendezvous because he had been killed in the war. Her ghost waits for him still. She makes cold breezes as she goes to the window in her futile watch, her phantom footsteps sounding on the floorboards. One guest who felt the cold breeze also heard a crinkling or rustling that sounded like someone in a skirt walking past.

Another story dating to colonial days concerns a horse thief said to have hidden at the tavern to escape pursuing Indians. He was given shelter until someone recognized him as a horse thief wanted by the law. Court was in session back then, and the thief was tried, convicted, sentenced, and executed by hanging, all in one-stop justice on site!

Each guest room has a diary, and many guests have left accounts of their ghostly experiences. Staff members also have their ghostly experiences to tell.

One night, employees returning to the empty tavern after hours saw through the windows a man sitting at the tavern bar drinking. Wondering how they could have left without seeing him, they hurried inside—only to find an empty bar. He may have been the same ghost seen over the years by patrons and staff—a man dressed in rough colonial garb who walks through the establishment, and sits at tables. A customer once described an odd-looking man in a flannel shirt sitting at a table. She observed him for some minutes, but when she looked away and looked back, the man had vanished.

Busy nights when the tavern is full of people enjoying themselves seem to draw out the ghosts. Phantoms dressed in period clothing have been seen standing around to listen to a very much alive piano player

Melissa Jacobs has had many encounters with strange phenomena while managing the establishment. Odd things happen with the door to the attic apartment. She finds it sometimes open, sometimes closed—alternately within minutes of the other—even though no one is on the attic level. She and other members of the staff sometimes feel presences, or feel like someone has lightly tapped or touched them. Objects get moved and misplaced. Napkins folded neatly on the tables are found mysteriously tossed about.

A couple who stayed overnight awakened in the middle of the night to hear their shower running in their bathroom. Each assumed the other had gotten up to take a shower. In the morning, they discovered that neither had. Who ran the shower? The only way in to the bathroom was through their locked bedroom door. Evidently one of the resident ghosts likes to stay clean!

According to the diaries, guests experience the unexplained slamming of doors in the middle of the night, creaking floorboards outside their rooms as though someone is walking past, and thumping noises above and below them. Muffled voices are heard coming from the attic area when no one is there, and the room is locked.

Guests in all four rooms have reported strange experiences. Room 3 is particularly active. One night the occupants awakened to see a ghostly woman in a skirt with a shawl over her head standing by the air conditioner. The apparition remained for several minutes and then vanished. On another occasion in Room 3, a guest reported, "Either the staff was playing tricks on us or a ghost thought we needed a drink, as we found several drinking straws pushed under our door this morning." There was no explanation for the straws. The husband said he heard rustling sounds and footsteps during the night.

The ghosts who frequent Room 3 also flush the toilet at night. And once the strong smell of freshly baked sugar cookies wafted through the room in the middle of the night, long after all the staff had gone home. The chandelier in the room has been seen to move and sway on its own. A woman was awakened by heavy footsteps thudding across the room, which stopped at her side of the bed. She felt an invisible presence prod her a few times and then leave.

Still other guests in Room 3 went outside one afternoon to enjoy their porch, when the door to their room slammed shut by itself. The door was locked, and they were unable to get back into their room. "It slammed so hard we all jumped out of our chairs," one guest wrote, noting that there was no breeze that day to account for the event. "Was it something we said?" she wondered, speculating on whether or not they had inadvertently offended an eavesdropping ghost.

In Room 4, a guest reported that a shirt he hung on a door hook before retiring at night was found in the morning with a large ragged hole in it. Another guest heard soft music during the night, at a time when the place was closed and empty of staff and entertainers.

A man spending the night in Room 4—and who said he was a skeptic about the paranormal—awakened to see a shadowy form on the porch outside the room. It appeared to be a tall, gaunt man in a long, flowing cape. He got up to investigate and looked outside. A long shadow slid off the rail, followed by a flapping sound like a flag whipping in the wind. "I told my wife about it this morning," he wrote. "She does not believe me."

Other guests in Room 4 heard a crash outside their room and found the rocking chairs upturned. "How do you spell poltergeist?" one wrote in the diary.

A woman in Room 4 heard footsteps outside the door in the

night and saw a shadow under the door. She could glimpse what appeared to be old brown boots. Whoever was wearing them departed—but made no sounds. "It was weird, very weird," she reported.

In Room 2, a woman reported that she felt a ghostly hand touch the back of her neck and move her long hair. There were crashing sounds in the room, and a knocking on the door—but no one was there when she opened the door. For another guest in Room 2, a thoughtful ghost picked a woman's handbag up off the floor and hung it on a coat hook. Still another guest awakened to see an apparition of a man wearing a long coat standing in the room.

A woman saw her husband walking down the hallway, followed by an apparition of a bearded man dressed in a uniform with three silver buttons. Later during the night, the rocking chair on the porch of Room 2 rocked by itself, and the doorknob to the locked room jingled as though someone were trying to enter. Another guest saw the outline of a soldier in uniform sitting in a chair in Room 2.

I made my first trip to the Jean Bonnet with members of the Center for Paranormal Study and Investigation (CPSI), based in Pittsburgh and founded by Tom Harter, president. We took all four guest rooms, and after the place closed at 11:00 P.M., we had the premises to ourselves for a nearly all-night investigation. The only place we could not access was the tavern room. We could, however, see into the tavern.

We recorded intriguing EVP in the hallway of the guest rooms. Scott Philips began getting activation of his EMF meter, apparently in response to questions. He asked the communicator to affect the meter again: "Can you come out—can you make it [the meter] go off again? Can you make it squeal like that?" When he played back his digital recording, we could all hear a female voice reply, "Sure I can." It was difficult to determine her age. Some of us thought it sounded like an elderly woman, while others, myself included, thought it sounded like a little girl.

All of us had quiet nights in our rooms once we were done investigating. I stayed in room 1 and kept a video surveillance going throughout the night. No ghosts passed in front of the camera. However, since we had performing ghosts for our equipment, it is not surprising that the energy level decreased by the time we retired between three and four in the morning.

The Jean Bonnet has plenty of ghostly phenomena, as the reports of guests and staff attest. If you plan an overnight visit, take the advice of one guest who wrote in the diary, "May I remind everyone to sleep with one eye open... Don't worry—the ghosts are all friendly."

And the food is fantastic.

CHAPTER 10

The Inn at Jim Thorpe
JIM THORPE

THE FIRST TIME I HEARD OF Jim Thorpe was in the 1990s, when I was visiting a friend in Allentown. Jim Thorpe seemed a most unusual and unlikely name for a town, a place I wanted to see. And on top of it, I was told the town was haunted. It was a must-see!

I have been back to Jim Thorpe several times, and it never ceases to enchant me. It is indeed rich in ghosts. A tiny place tucked into what is called the Anthracite District in Pennsylvania, Jim Thorpe seems genuinely stuck in an earlier time. The Inn at Jim Thorpe has witnessed the town's entire history, and along the way has collected a few resident ghosts.

Set in the steep Pocono Mountains along the Lehigh River, the town had its beginnings under the bland name of Coalville. By 1815, it was a growing settlement, and in 1816 its name was changed to Mauch Chunk, an Indian term meaning "Bear Mountain." Coal mining was the big industry, and entrepreneurs came here to build their fortunes. Soon, the town was a coal transportation center and it became the Carbon County seat.

To accommodate the thousands of visitors to Mauch Chunk, Cornelius Connor built the White Swan Hotel in 1833. Large and rambling, it was one of several hotels in town. But in 1849, a great fire swept the commercial district, and the White Swan was one of the many buildings that burned to the ground. Connor rebuilt it and renamed it the New American Hotel.

In the nineteenth century, Mauch Chunk boomed as a tourist town, attracting more visitors than any other destination except Niagara Falls. It was known as "the Switzerland of America." People came to see the Switchback Gravity Railroad and Glen Onoko Falls. That era of prosperity ended in the 1930s with the onset of the Great Depression. The entire town of Mauch Chunk fell on hard times.

The hotel languished until the 1980s, when it was purchased by John Drury, who restored it to its New Orleans–style grandeur. Since 1988 it has been known as the Inn at Jim Thorpe. The hotel is a landmark for the visitors who pass through. People come now to see tourist attractions, enjoy the Poconos scenery, and stroll the streets lined with quaint shops.

How did the name of the town change from Mauch Chunk to Jim Thorpe? After the Depression, Mauch Chunk still struggled to find a new economy. Coal mining had declined. Tourism remained promising, but the town needed a fresh identity.

In 1953 the great athlete Jim Thorpe died in Philadelphia. Thorpe, born in 1888, was of Native American (Fox and Sauk) blood. He played basketball, baseball, and football. In 1912, he set a record for the decathlon in the Summer Olympics in Stockholm, Sweden. After his death, his widow sought to have a memorial erected for him in his native state of Oklahoma, but was unsuccessful. She found the citizens of Mauch Chunk more than willing to champion the athlete—they were willing to have the entire town named after him. In February 1954, Thorpe's body was relocated to a mausoleum on the east side of town. The publicity gave the town an economic shot in the arm.

The Inn has hosted many dignitaries over the last couple of centuries including Presidents Ulysses S. Grant and William H. Taft as well as Buffalo Bill, Thomas Edison, and John D. Rockefeller.

Jim Thorpe is a ghost enthusiast's paradise. It is said that if you walk the streets at night, you will be surrounded by ghosts. Many ghost stories abound, and while the streets may not literally teem with them, the odds are good that you will have some mysterious experience if you spend some time here.

At the inn, guests have reported unexplained activity in many of the rooms. Much of it centers on poltergeist-like pranks, such as moving objects and making banging noises. Guests have also seen shadows in the downstairs foyer and lobby.

Room 211 is the most haunted room. A figure of a faceless woman in Victorian dress wanders through the room and disappears into the closet, and guests have awakened to find the room inexplicably and severely cold. The TV goes on and off by itself. Men seem to be haunted more than women, and find that their belongings disappear and then reappear in odd spots. One man left his boots by the door when he went to sleep. Upon awakening, he found them in the hallway outside. Towels are found shoved in the toilet. One can smell cigar and cigarette smoke when nobody is there or hear the laughter of invisible children.

Also on the second floor, Room 203 has similar activity.

One guest reported that a ghost put his cell phone in the refrigerator.

On the third floor, Room 303 sports unexplainable shadows and orbs of light that move about. Room 310 is believed to be haunted by a nurse who still tends her patient. She becomes irritated when guests climb into the bed that is supposed to be occupied by her patient. She appears at bedside as a white figure, and sometime she grabs the unsuspecting sleepers with an icy grip. A phantom man with slicked back hair also appears in Room 310. Room 315 has chairs that are found turned upside down.

I stayed in Room 211 on one occasion. In the middle of the night I was awakened by the sound of the bathroom doorknob rattling, as though someone were turning it back and forth. No one, of course, was there.

I also spent time in one of the sitting areas in the hallway on the second floor, hoping to catch a glimpse of the faceless woman or ghostly figures that might walk past. I had no sightings, but I did speak with a guest who had been to the inn several times and said she often felt followed by someone invisible when going to her room on the second floor at night.

The town of Jim Thorpe has many other ghostly sites to visit. Be sure to take in the Old Jail Museum, which used to be the Carbon County Prison, profiled in the next chapter.

CHAPTER 11

The Old Jail Museum
JIM THORPE

THE MOST HAUNTED SITE in the historic coal mining town of Jim Thorpe is the former Carbon County Prison, now known as the Old Jail Museum. No longer a working prison, it was the scene of controversial executions that took place in the 1870s, in which seven innocent men may have been hanged without just cause. Numerous other executions took place in the jail during the course of its history, and visitors experience a wide range of paranormal phenomena during tours. Staff members have also had many experiences. The jail is most famous for a mysterious hand print of a condemned man that allegedly cannot be washed away, painted over, or even chiseled out.

Constructed of hand-cut stone, the jail was completed in 1871. It was designed by Edward Haviland, the son of John Haviland, who designed Eastern State Penitentiary in Philadelphia. The Carbon County Prison had seventy-two rooms, including a warden's living quarters, twenty-five cells in the main block on the first and second floors, sixteen cells in the dungeon, and three cells for women on the second floor. The customary means of execution was by hanging, and a large and ominous-looking gallows was constructed for that purpose in the main cell block.

The prison was in operation until 1995. Tom and Betty Lou McBride of Jim Thorpe purchased it, restored it, and turned it into a museum. The McBrides collected hundreds of mysterious experiences reported to them over the years.

Only a few years after the prison opened, it became the center of controversy over a case known as "the Molly Maguires." Jim Thorpe, which was known in those days by its Indian name of Mauch Chunk, had attracted a large number of Irish immigrants who worked in the coal mines. Working conditions in the mines were dreadful and the miners were paid poorly. A secret society calling itself the Molly Maguires began to push for reform. The Molly Maguires had actually formed in Ireland to battle unscrupulous landlords; the group took its name from a woman who was at the forefront of protest. In America, the Molly Maguires took on the challenge of confronting the coal lords. The Mollies were vigilantes and tried to organize a union, which was crushed by the coal companies.

In 1875 coal boss John P. Jones was murdered. Seven coal miners were arrested, tried, and found guilty. They were all hanged between 1877 and 1879. They all protested their innocence to the very end, and many today believe they were indeed framed. On December 5, 2005, the Pennsylvania State House of Representatives passed a resolution recognizing the lack of due process for several of the men.

The first of the doomed men were hanged on June 21, 1877:

Alexander Campbell, Edward Kelly, Michael Doyle, and John Donohue. Thomas P. Fisher was hanged on March 28, 1878, and James McDonnell and Charles Sharpe were hanged on January 14, 1879.

Another accused Mollie, James Kerrigan, was arrested and put in the prison dungeon along with Kelly. Kerrigan turned state's evidence and testified against his fellow miners, for which his family was compensated in the amount of one thousand dollars. After his release, Kerrigan changed his name and took his family out of the state, probably to avoid revenge.

According to lore, one of the first doomed men placed his hand on the yellowed wall of Cell 17 and proclaimed that his hand print would stay there permanently as testimony to his innocence. Campbell and Fisher have been the two favored candidates, but many visitors coming through the jail have been prompted—by ghosts?—to announce that the print belongs to Doyle.

Supposedly, the dark gray print has resisted destruction. A stone mason, Albertus Herman, chiseled it out four times in the late 1920s and in the 1930s, and the hand was said to mysteriously return. Some doubt its authenticity, however. Nonetheless, it is one of the star attractions of the museum, and many people attest to a lot of haunting phenomena in and around Cell 17. Visitors pick up on intense anger and some see the apparition of a man. Some are overcome with odd feelings and rush out of the prison. Cells 6 and 25 also are focal points of similar oppressive haunting phenomena, such as bad feelings and heavy physical sensations.

Throughout the prison museum, people see apparitions of men and women. On the second floor, visitors have been pushed by a strong invisible force that prevents them from moving forward. People have had their clothing tugged, sometimes violently. Cameras fail to work. Phantom voices reverberate throughout the building. Shadows, flashing lights, and misty clouds move about.

Perhaps the oddest phantom voice was a woman screaming, "I'm too late! I'm too late!" which a visitor heard as she went up the stairs to the second floor of the main cell block. The visitor did not know that a real story corroborated the voice. In 1879, Charles Sharpe's wife was working feverishly for a reprieve for her husband. As execution day drew near, she appealed to the state governor. On the day of Sharpe's hanging, the governor granted a five-day reprieve for Sharpe and McDonnell. Mrs. Sharpe raced to the prison, but she was refused entry and the men were hanged. After the men were dead, she was allowed in. She raced up the stairs screaming, "I'm too late! I'm too late!"

Staff and visitors have seen shadowy figures, heard ghostly bagpipe music, women crying and wailing, and even the sounds of invisible persons playing cards. In what is now the library on the second floor, people have reported being pushed and kicked and feeling negative presences. Books have been moved about without explanation.

The gallows on display are recreations, but are erected in the same place as the originals. Many visitors feel choked and suffocated when they approach them.

In the dungeon, visitors feel anger, sadness and despair, and some sense the pain of beatings and torture. Headaches, dizziness, and strange physical feelings are often reported. An apparition of a man with his leg cut off—possibly due to gangrene—has been seen sitting in one of the cells. Volunteer guides do not like being in the dungeon alone, according to the McBrides.

The former Carbon County Prison is tiny compared to monster facilities such as Eastern State Penitentiary, but it packs a lot of exotic history and paranormal bang for the space. It is hard to leave the place without feeling touched in some way by the life-and-death dramas that took place here, some of which seem to have left their mark forever.

CHAPTER 12

Greater Johnstown/ Cambria County Convention and Visitors Bureau

JOHNSTOWN

IN 1889, JOHNSTOWN WAS HIT with a sudden and massive flood that took two thousand lives and destroyed the downtown of the city. The devastation was beyond belief, and the entire region was in shock. The city eventually recovered and rebuilt, and life went on. But for many of those whose lives had ended, a ghostly twilight ensued. Some of the victims lingered on, perhaps out of confusion. Some might have been angry at dying in a disaster that many had warned was only a matter of time before it happened. Others might have stayed on to search for loved ones torn away from them in the raging flood waters. Whatever the reasons, Johnstown is still haunted by this tragedy more than a century later, by guilt, by grief—and by ghosts.

Founded in 1800, Johnstown had always had a problem with water. It was built at the confluence of Little Stony Creek and Little Conemaugh River, forming the Conemaugh River, an area always prone to flooding. As its importance in the steel industry grew, the riverbed above the city was narrowed, further exacerbating the flooding from the rain and snow runoffs from the steep hills of the Conemaugh Valley and Allegheny Mountains. Just downstream from Johnstown, the river narrowed naturally for ten miles due to plunging mountainsides.

From 1838 to 1853, the state undertook the construction of the South Fork Dam, located in South Fork high upriver from Johnstown. The dam was intended to be part of a canal and reservoir system that would supply water to Johnstown and provide canal barge transportation for industry. The development of railroads made that obsolete, and the reservoir was abandoned by the state.

Industrialist Henry Clay Frick—whose haunted mansion in Pittsburgh is a historical home—led a group of investors to purchase the reservoir and turn it into Lake Conemaugh, a pleasure place for the rich. When it was finished, the four-hundred-acre lake held twenty million tons of water. But the alterations made for boating and fishing made the dam more vulnerable to leakages and breaks, which happened repeatedly.

The exclusive lake club opened in 1881. Whenever the dam leaked, it was patched up with mud and straw. There was little concern for the safety of the residents below the dam, who were primarily working class German and Welsh immigrants feeding the lifestyles of the rich and famous who used the lake club.

In late May of 1889, the region was soaked by days of heavy rains. The dam swelled dangerously near its top. On May 31, water leaked out and began to flood down the Little Conemaugh

River, filling the streets of Johnstown up to ten feet high. The walls of the dam eroded, and desperate attempts were made to keep them from breaking. At 3:10 P.M. on May 31, the dam burst, and twenty million tons of water went racing down the narrow river. It took only forty minutes for the entire lake to drain.

The floodwaters hit the towns of South Fork and East Conemaugh, wreaking devastation and killing a few dozen people. Trees, buildings, barbed wire from a factory and other debris were swept into the torrent that then descended upon Johnstown at forty miles an hour. The citizens were caught by surprise. Some were able to scramble to safety, but thousands were drowned or crushed by the water.

The flood was the worst flood disaster of the century, destroying sixteen hundred homes and four square miles of downtown Johnstown. The property damage mounted to seventeen million dollars; the city spent years cleaning up the mess.

Clara Barton had just founded the American Red Cross in 1881, and the Great Flood of Johnstown was the organization's first big disaster. She set up a clinic and morgue in an Episcopal church, and stayed in town for five months.

The Reverend David Beale, pastor of the First Presbyterian Church, was another important figure during relief efforts. Eight other temporary morgues were set up, including Beale's church, and he began compiling a "Book of the Dead" with information about the corpses that would help family and friends identify them. Beale also started detailed diaries about the flood, and took numerous photographs—activities that later became controversial and may have played a role in the hauntings attributed to him today.

In all, Beale compiled three books of the dead, which made notes of teeth, tattoos, body marks, and so on. About 770 victims were never positively identified. If there are restless dead in Johnstown, they are the best candidates. He filled about thirty diaries and began writing a memoir.

In 1890, barely a year after the disaster, Beale left town, almost run out by angry citizens who claimed he refused to allow the public access to his records. He was accused of writing a memoir in order to profit on the tragedy. Beale was outraged by these accusations. Even prior to the flood, he had been a controversial figure in town, but he had in all sincerity acted heroically in the aftermath of the flood. Ousted by his church, he moved to Frederick, Maryland, and then to Philadelphia. He remained bitter about his treatment for the rest of his life.

Beale's spirit is still strong in Johnstown, and many say he haunts the entire city, especially the old area devastated by the flood. His presence is especially strong at the Greater Johnstown/Cambria County Convention and Visitors Bureau, which envelops his old First Presbyterian Church. The church is now privately owned and is an abandoned theater. If you visit the bureau, pay attention while you are browsing the tourist literature. A ghost may be looking over your shoulder.

Mick Retort, the founder of the Watchful Eye Paranormal Study group of Pittsburgh, has visited Johnstown a number of times. "I have a fascination with Johnstown—the whole place is comfortably eerie," he said. "You can feel it in the atmosphere."

At the bureau, cameras have malfunctioned. People hear strange knocking sounds and unintelligible voices, some of which whisper in people's ears. Some visitors feel dizzy and have spells of confusion. There are unexplained cold spots. People feel watched and hear phantom footsteps. Occasionally, there is a whiff of an unpleasant odor, such as might be expected in a morgue. Phantom moaning sounds are heard. Drawers in the offices are found open when rooms have been locked and empty. Sounds emanate from empty offices.

It is said that Reverend Beale is causing most of the phenomena. His ghost is occasionally seen, looking haggard as though he is rushing about tending to victims. "He is still there watching over the place," said Retort. "He doesn't want to let go."

SOUTHERN
PENNSYLVANIA

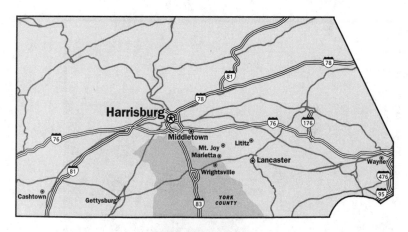

Cashtown
  Cashtown Inn

Gettysburg
  Gettysburg Battlefield and
  Environs

Lancaster
  Fulton Opera House

Lititz
  General Sutter Inn

Marietta
  The Railroad House

Middletown
  Alfred's Victorian Restaurant

Mt. Joy
  Bube's Brewery

Wayne
  The Grave of Mad Anthony Wayne

Wrightsville
  Accomac Inn

York County
  Chickie's Rock
  Cordorus Furnace

CHAPTER 13

Gettysburg Battlefield and Environs

GETTYSBURG

BARELY A SCRAP OF EARTH on the huge battlefield at Gettysburg is not haunted. A person can spend years doing research here, and some paranormal investigators have done just that. Even the best of them, however, say they still haven't covered it all. I lived near Gettysburg for a little more than a decade and made frequent trips there for research and investigation. From a paranormal perspective, the place is fascinating, and always full of surprises.

The tide of the Civil War turned here in fighting from July 1-3, 1863. Up to that point, the Confederates had the edge, and the situation didn't look so good for the Union. Neither side intended to fight at Gettysburg, and the battle happened by a confluence of unexpected circumstances. General Robert E. Lee decided to send his Confederate troops northward to divert attention from the Southern capital established in Richmond, Virginia. His men were also in need of supplies. Near Gettysburg, they encountered Union forces commanded by General George Meade, who were moving north in search of Lee. Each having met the enemy, they engaged in battle.

The fighting was bloody and intense. Those words could describe many a Civil War battlefield, but Gettysburg stands out. Survivors of the battle and the war said Gettysburg was the only place where they saw the blood and gore run in rivulets.

Approximately 165,000 men fought and 50,000 were casualties—more than the residents of the entire little town of Gettysburg. The residents were caught off guard, and fled for their lives in the hail of bullets. Amazingly, only one civilian was killed—Jenny Wade, cut down instantly by a stray bullet that shot through her sister's house where Jenny was baking bread.

For two days, the battle raged back and forth in a carnage of blood. On the third day of fighting, Lee made a fatal mistake. He decided to hit the center of the Union line by sending twelve thousand men across an open field toward the Union-held Cemetery Ridge. It was a suicide mission. The Confederates were exposed and vulnerable in the open field and were easily cut down by Union troops behind the shelter of the ridge. It was like shooting fish in a barrel. Most of the twelve thousand died in the field. One of the generals who led the charge was George Pickett. The suicide mission became known as Pickett's Charge.

On July 4, both sides waited for each other to attack. Lee wisely assessed his weakened position and retreated on July 5, with Meade in pursuit. From then on, it was downhill for the South, and two years later, in 1865, the Confederacy surrendered.

While the armies were still preoccupied with fighting, the civilians had to contend with the wreckage left behind. In addition to the tens of thousands of bodies, there were about five thousand dead and rotting horses, and the ruins caused by shelling. Farms and homes were damaged and destroyed. Many had been taken over as housing for troops and for hospitals. The wounded and dying were everywhere, and their amputated limbs piled in the streets and outside homes.

In a way, Gettysburg never really recovered. The town and landscape were eventually cleaned up, the dead were buried or taken away for burial, and people went on about their lives and business. But the dead have never rested in peace, and Gettysburg is one extremely active haunted place.

Mark Nesbitt is a former park ranger at Gettysburg who now runs the leading ghost tour business there, the Ghosts of Gettysburg Tours. Nesbitt almost singlehandedly put Gettysburg on the ghost map, writing a series of guidebooks on the hauntings there. Nesbitt and his wife, Carol, are excellent investigators, and the most reliable sources for anything paranormal concerning Gettysburg.

"All the elements are here for a good haunting," Nesbitt told me. "You have sudden death, violent death, youthful death, and unconsecrated burials. The soldiers were pretty much buried in shallow graves right where they fell. The Union soldiers were moved to cemeteries within a few months, but the Confederates lay in the ground until 1870-71, when their families could raise enough money to bring them home. There was also a lot of fear of God's judgment going on during the battle. There were a lot of Christian revivals during the Civil War. The soldiers knew they were committing mortal sin when they pulled the trigger.

"I think the emotional factor was there, too. Every soldier there knew this was a big battle. The Confederates were at the apex of their power, and the Union troops knew they had to stop them. A lot of Pennsylvanians were fighting on their own soil."

Almost anywhere you go on the battlefield, you will find residual activity, that is, imprints of ghosts of the dead who constantly reenact the battle. Visitors hear gunfire, shouting, screaming, marching, drumming, running, and panicked horses. There are sounds of music and conversation, and phantom lights where campfires once illuminated the darkness. There are active ghosts, too, who communicate via EVP and other phenomena and sometimes show up in photographs.

You can get a good feel for the battlefield by dropping in at the recently renovated Visitor's Center, which offers a spectacular documentary of the battle presented in a Cyclorama. It also has a museum and well-stocked store that sells gifts and books. Bus tour tickets can be purchased there, too. Hours of operation vary according to season, so check ahead.

You can pick up free maps to take your own driving tour, which enables you to stop and linger to suit your needs. You can take your investigation gear into the battlefield. The park is closed at dusk, and investigators are not welcome to prowl the park in the dark. The park service patrols the area and has the right to confiscate your film or equipment if you are found trespassing.

Many of the buildings in town are haunted with Civil War ghosts. Some of the old farmhouses have been turned into bed-and-breakfast inns, and they are haunted, too.

Here are a few of the highlights of Gettysburg haunts. If you have limited time, zero in on these:

Devil's Den

The name Devil's Den says it all, embodying the evil of war and the horrors war leaves behind. Devil's Den is a hot spot, where important fighting left the rocky ground strewn with twisted bodies.

Most of the fighting here took place on July 1 and 2. Union

troops were barricaded atop a hill called Little Round Top. Confederate sharpshooters in the little valley below were hidden in snake-infested rocks and boulders. After the fighting was over, Confederate bodies were everywhere in the rock crevices. Some of the dead were left in the crevices and were never buried. Apparitions of soldiers were reported soon after the armies were gone. Sightings continue into the present.

Supposedly some of the bodies found there were determined not to have died from bullet wounds, fostering rumors that they had been killed supernaturally. Most likely, they were killed by severe concussions caused by the hellish roar of cannon fire ricocheting off the rocks.

Devil's Den actually was known as a haunted place long before the Civil War. The Gettysburg locals called it a "desolate and ghostly place" haunted by Indians who had fought there. Early white settlers had seen apparitions of Indians and heard them hollering and whooping.

People who have taken photographs around Devil's Den are sometimes surprised to find "extras" in them—figures of men in old uniforms or even ragged clothing (typical of some of the poorly dressed troops of the time) standing among the rocks. Apparitions have also been seen. The best time to catch phenomena is dusk.

THE TRIANGULAR FIELD

At the bottom of Devil's Den is an odd little field shaped like a triangle, hence the name. For its size, it is extraordinarily haunted. "If you only have an hour to do ghosthunting at Gettysburg, the Triangular Field is probably it," said Nesbitt.

The Triangular Field officially got its name in the 1970s due to its odd shape. Nesbitt was first to bring attention to the paranormal stuff there. "There's some kind of vortex in that area that seems to take care of cameras and batteries," he said, noting that cameras of all kinds often suddenly lose their battery power when taken into the field and mysteriously regain it when they are taken out. Dowsing rods also go crazy. So unusual are the effects, said Nesbitt, "I thought there was a lodestone there. But it is as ordinary geologically as your backyard."

People whose cameras continue to work have sometimes captured images of dark figures moving in the woods behind the field.

Nesbitt has an idea why cameras go haywire more here than on most other sites in the battlefield. After the fighting was over, photographers who came in to photograph the carnage wanted something dramatic. Matthew Brady, who became famous for his battlefield photographs, had the corpse of a young Confederate soldier dragged from the Triangular Field and propped up in the boulders of Devil's Den, along with a rifle. The photograph was billed as a Southern sharpshooter slain in Devil's Den by Union forces. "If there is anybody who has reason to be angry at photographers, it's him," said Nesbitt.

EVPs are common in the Triangular Field. In fact, Nesbitt got his first EVP there. "I stood in the middle of this field in the pitch dark and asked, 'Is there anybody here with me?' I had the recorder on voice activation. As soon as I asked, I thought, 'Boy do I feel stupid.' Then the numbers on the recorder started moving. On playback, I got roars and hisses and a voice that sounded like it said 'Yes.' That launched me on the EVP part of my career. Nesbitt has collected more than one thousand EVPs, most of them at Gettysburg.

IVERSON'S PITS

Was it carelessness or bad judgment, or a combination of both, that sent nearly fifteen hundred Confederate men on a suicide march on July 1, 1863? Their ghosts have plenty to say in whispers and EVP in the field where the men fell like dolls and were buried—Iverson's Pits.

The pits take their name from Brigadier General Alfred Iverson of North Carolina. On that fateful day, Iverson was to be joined by two other brigades in an attack on Union forces behind a stone wall on Oak Ridge. To get there, they had to cross the open fields of the John S. Forney farm.

One of the supporting brigades, under the command of General O'Neal of Alabama, attacked too early and was driven back. This exposed Iverson's brigade, but he nonetheless ordered his men to advance and "give them hell." Unfortunately, hell was visited upon the Confederates. The Union men could hardly believe that Iverson handed over his men on a platter, making their way unprotected across open space, as though no one had surveyed the landscape in advance. The Union fire mowed them down—dozens of them fell in straight lines. The dead and missing were numbered between 750 and 820, according to different reports.

Iverson's men were buried where they fell. In the 1870s, what little remained of their corpses were taken home to the South. But not all of them went home. The shallow depression known as Iverson's Pits is rich in ghostly phenomena, especially voices recorded in EVP. Some give their names, some tell how they died, some keep reliving that fateful day.

THE WHEATFIELD

Wheat fields were everywhere in the Gettysburg area in Civil War days, but one small field stands out, and is simply known as "The Wheatfield" or the "Rose Wheatfield." On July 2, 1863, it was the scene of some of the bloodiest fighting of the war. When the smoke cleared, the entire field was soaked in blood, and the living could scarcely walk through the field without stepping on corpses.

BALADERRY INN

The Baladerry Inn was one of the many private farm homes taken over by Union troops during the battle, and used as a makeshift hospital. Today it is a bed-and-breakfast. Every guest room is said to have activity, and after spending a weekend there myself with a group of paranormal investigators, I agree.

The Baladerry is a gracious brick Federal-style home dating to about 1830. It has three buildings, an old house, main house, and carriage house, where the barn used to be. The property is set on lovely grounds covering four acres at the edge of the battlefield, within walking distance of Little Round Top, Devil's Den, and the Wheatfield. The original wooden floor of the dining room still has bloodstains from wounded soldiers.

I stayed in the carriage house in a ground-floor room to the right of the front door. In the middle of the night, I was awakened by the sounds of loud scraping, which seemed to be coming from overhead. The noises sounded like heavy furniture or boxes being dragged across the floor. The racket went on for some time, as though people were moving things one way, then back, then back again.

I thought the perpetrators were fellow investigators who had come in very late. "What on earth are they doing, and why do they have to do it now?" I wondered in irritation as I tried to get back to sleep.

The next morning, I found out who was staying in the room overhead and demanded to know why they had felt a need to push heavy things around at 3:00 A.M. They were astonished. They, too, had heard the noise—and thought it was coming from below. From me! In fact, everyone staying the carriage house had heard it, and thought it was caused by someone else.

The same racket occurred on the second night at the same time.

Sounds of heavy objects being pushed across floors is a common haunting phenomenon. Why do ghosts like to drag invisible furniture around? Who knows!

I also was awakened by a tapping on my front window—but no one was there when I looked out. I learned later that others who stayed in that room reported the same thing.

Most startling of all was a photograph I took that showed the ghostly forms of a boy and girl, captured in the side window. I was walking around the grounds during the day taking random photographs, and I snapped shots of my windows. Ghosts sometimes show up in reflective surfaces. When I looked at my images, a chill shot through me as I saw the obvious figures of the children in the glass. They looked like they were dressed in period clothing. The boy was clutching something like a box or small case. The girl was taller and standing behind him and had something in her hair, like a ribbon or small bonnet. Were they the ghost children of a family who once stayed there or perhaps lived there? There was no answer to be found. But they were captured in the glass, looking out from my room.

In the main house, a male ghost likes to visit ladies at night, and some of the female investigators staying there said they sensed a presence in their room or felt invisible fingers playing with their hair.

LADY FARM

One of the strangest paranormal stories to come out of Gettysburg happened at the Daniel Lady Farm. The farm, like most of the private homes and farms in the Gettysburg area, was turned into a hospital for the Confederate wounded. The stone house and barn were used as a Confederate field hospital. General Edward "Allegheny" Johnson, division commander, used the stone house as his division headquarters. Johnson's division listed 1,269 wounded. Burials were recorded on the site.

The 140-acre farm is now owned by the Gettysburg Battlefield Preservation Association and is not open to the public, but can be accessed by specially arranged tours and investigations conducted by the Nesbitts. If your trip to Gettysburg coincides with one of their Lady Farm events, it is well worth including in your itinerary.

The front room of the old house served as the operating room, and bloodstains are still on the floorboards. Apparitions have been seen in the house, and EVP activity is high. Out in the barn, the wounded and dying were laid in rows on the ground.

On my first visit to the Lady Farm, I concentrated on the barn with medium Laine Crosby, who works with the Nesbitts. We saw apparitions of the some of the soldiers, and also a figure in white moving among them. I had the feeling that it was an angel of death who was ministering to the dying. A moving but chilling experience.

But let's get back to the strangest experience probably ever documented at Gettysburg. One afternoon, Mark Nesbitt received a phone call from the Lady Farm caretaker. "Mark, if you want to see a paranormal event happening right before your eyes, come on out," he said.

Nesbitt quickly threw his investigation gear into his car, and within a few minutes was knocking on the front door of the farm house. The caretaker opened it and said cryptically, "I'm not going to say anything, we're just going to go in."

They went into the front room, where operations had taken place. Right in front of the fireplace, where the operating table would have been, were four or five long, rust-colored streaks of liquid flowing from the middle of the floor toward the fireplace. Separating from them was a clear serum. Around the serum were rust-colored drops that looked like they were starting to crystallize.

Nesbitt was momentarily thrown off and wondered if an old pipe had burst, but there was no sign of anything amiss in the ceiling.

"This just appeared," the caretaker said, pointing to the streams.

Nesbitt measured the streams, which were about five to six feet in length. He took photographs and videos of them. Then he asked for a tissue, dipped it in the rust-colored liquid, and put it in a plastic bag.

The caretaker then said he had to return to work, so Nesbitt left. About two hours later, the caretaker called him to say that the liquids had mysteriously vanished as abruptly as they had appeared.

Nesbitt returned to the Lady Farm. The liquids had indeed vanished. All that remained was a thin layer of dust.

The Nesbitts sent the soaked tissue to one of the most prestigious forensics labs in the country. About three weeks later, the results came back: The substance was human blood!

Nesbitt remains at a loss to explain the phenomena. "To this day, you can see the bloodstains on the floor from the operating," he said. "You cannot get them out. Yet this blood was not only completely gone, there was a thin layer of dust left behind that had not been there before. It was like time went in reverse."

CHAPTER 14

Cashtown Inn

CASHTOWN

THIS ELEGANT EIGHTEENTH-CENTURY INN on the Lincoln Highway (Old 30) about eight miles outside of Gettysburg is a favorite of both Civil War buffs and ghost enthusiasts alike. The inn is rich in both history and hauntings. Some historians hold that this is the place where the South really lost the war, because of decisions made here in the fateful summer of 1863.

Apparently, there are still ghosts around to testify to that, for patrons tell of being touched by unseen hands, seeing apparitions, and hearing strange, disembodied voices. Ghost experiences date back to the late nineteenth century, and guests have been reporting similar phenomena ever since.

The Cashtown Inn was built around 1797. It was the first stagecoach stop west of Gettysburg on the Gettysburg-Chambersburg Pike. It quickly became famous as *the* place to stay for good food, drink, and lodging. But innkeeper Peter Marks was a hardline businessman, and he accepted only cash—no credit or bartered goods. Thus, the inn became known as the Cashtown Inn. The tiny town of Cashtown developed around the inn.

Prior to the battle of Gettysburg, fought from July 1-3, 1863, Robert E. Lee's Army of Northern Virginia had spread across southern Pennsylvania without resistance. Late on June 28, Lee learned that the Union army was north of the Potomac River and was heading his way. Lee ordered his scattered army to concentrate at Cashtown, which stood strategically on his supply line back to Virginia, but to hold fast.

On June 29 , Lieutenant General Ambrose P. Hill and his officers made the inn their headquarters. Hill led the Third Corps of the Confederate Army. The troops camped in the nearby vicinity. It is said that more Confederate generals stayed at the Cashtown Inn in those few days than at any other house in America. There was tension in the air, for the Confederates knew the Union troops were somewhere close, and that a battle was imminent.

On June 30, General J. Johnston Pettigrew and his troops were out scouting around and encountered Union troops. They withdrew without confrontation, and Pettigrew reported back to his commander, Major General Henry Heth, stationed at the inn. Heth was itching for battle and needed a reason to get his troops out. Heth asked Hill if the general had any objection if he took his men out the next day to look for shoes for the troops. Hill replied, "None in the world." Thus, the fateful decision was made that led to battle the next day. Legend holds that many of the Confederate troops were barefoot, and Heth was actually looking for shoes. Footwear was but an excuse to go out and search for Union troops.

During the fighting, the inn, like many homes and farms, was turned into a makeshift hospital for the wounded. They were carried to the basement, where extreme surgeries such as limb amputations were performed. Chloroform, the only pain killer, was in short supply, and many amputations had to be done without benefit of anesthesia. The basement was filled with the screams of the wounded and the moans of the dying.

The original kitchen is in the basement, where a cold spring once provided all the cooking and drinking water for the inn. When the surgeries took place, surgeons dipped their blades in the spring water. The amputated limbs were thrown out a back door. Lore has it that so many limbs piled up that they completely blocked a window next to the door.

The Cashtown Inn is still in operation much as it was in the past. In 1996 it was purchased by Dennis and Eileen Hoover, who placed diaries in all the rooms for guests to record their comments. Many of the testimonies describe ghostly experiences. Shortly after moving into the inn, the Hoovers were awakened one night by a loud crash. Thinking it was an auto accident, they rushed to look out the window. The crash, however, was caused by all of their books on the top shelf of a bookcase being tossed to the floor.

Jack and Marie Paladino bought the inn in January 2006 and undertook major renovations on the first floor. Jack was skeptical about the ghosts and hauntings, but Marie was a believer. Today the Paladinos embrace the inn's haunted legacy and promote special ghost weekends in conjunction with Mark Nesbitt's Ghosts of Gettysburg tours and special events.

The basement where the surgeries were performed is off-limits to most guests, but those who participate in the ghost weekends can access it. In what is now the boiler room, people have reported seeing visions from the past: two Civil War soldiers attending a mortally wounded comrade. Numerous EVPs have been recorded in the basement.

Upstairs, activity has been reported in all the seven guest rooms (four bedrooms and three suites). Lights go on and off inexplicably in several rooms. EVP has been captured throughout the inn, especially upstairs. Guests hear rapping on their doors, but open them to find no one present. Intense cold spots manifest everywhere.

Room 2, named after Brigadier General John Imboden, has a ghost who likes to move jewelry and objects and also breathe heavily on guests. The radio has turned off by itself, and air conditioners have mysteriously been turned off in the middle of the night.

Room 3, the Lieutenant General Ambrose P. Hill room, is particularly active. This room was occupied by Hill for three days before the start of the battle. A chair in a corner reportedly moves on its own. People who sleep in the four-poster bed reportedly have their legs touched. A figure has been reported moving across the foot of the bed into the bathroom. Guests are awakened by strange, unexplained bangs and noises. The bathroom door is found opened on its own, and unseen hands tamper with the air conditioning. Phantom fiddle music has been heard. Also significant is a shadowy figure of man wearing a coat and hat who leaps over the bed and vanishes.

In Room 4, named after Major General Henry Heth, a ghost soldier in a Confederate uniform has been seen. He is believed to be a young man who was mortally wounded on the pike near the inn in June, just prior to the battle. The ghost is also seen in the hallways and standing in a doorway leading to the back of the bar on the first floor.

Activity in Room 5, the General Robert E. Lee Suite on the third floor, has sent people away in the middle of the night, according to the Paladinos. A rocking chair has been seen to move on its own. Guests have heard breathing and scratching at the window and have been touched. People on the floor below hear footsteps walking about when no one is in the room, and the staff find objects moved about.

Ghostly figures have been seen in the tavern side, especially near the bar entrance.

Mark Nesbitt has investigated the phenomena and the Cashtown Inn on many occasions, and hosts haunted weekends there. He told me about a group of archaeologists who stayed there and experienced particularly odd phenomena. They came downstairs in the morning and said that in the middle of the night, they had been disturbed by the sounds of horses snorting and pawing the ground outside. Looking out their windows, they saw nothing. They also commented that their suitcases were packed and wondered if the staff had done it. The neat helper was a ghost!

My first visit to the inn was as a participant in one of Mark Nesbitt's haunted weekend events. After a delicious dinner and introduction by Jack and Mark, we explored the inn. The basement was active for EVP. I also sensed a Confederate soldier ghost in Room 6, the Major General William D. Pender Suite, which is located above the basement area used as a makeshift hospital.

The Cashtown Inn is famous for its photograph of an "extra" taken in 1896. An extra is an unknown face or figure not seen when a photograph is taken, but who appears when film is developed or a photograph is examined.

Someone went across the road to photograph the building and a real man in front of it. The extra is a man wearing what appears to be Confederate army garb, a slouch hat, and an oversized shell jacket worn by the infantry. The figure is blurry, which means it may have been moving—or simply just out of this world. The other man is sharp and clear, and seems unaware of the extra. The photograph has never been debunked. You can see this famous photograph on display. The Paladinos also have a collection of unusual photographs sent to them by guests.

CHAPTER 15

Fulton Opera House
LANCASTER

PERFORMING ARTS CENTERS have more than their
fair share of ghosts. So do prisons. Combine the two and you
have an unusual haunting mix. You'll find it at the Fulton Opera
House in Lancaster.

To understand the haunted history of the opera house, one
must start in 1763 when the Lancaster jail was housing fourteen
Conestoga Indians. The Indians were not there for crimes, but
for safekeeping. The Conestoga, also known as the Susquehannock, were peaceful people who were gradually converting to
the white man's religion, Christianity. In 1701, they had signed
a treaty with William Penn to be of "one Head & One Heart, &
live in true Friendship & Amity as one People." Still, they were

96

hated by some white settlers, such as the Paxton Boys, a notorious gang of vigilantes who sought to wipe out the Conestogas.

On December 14, 1763, the Paxton Boys descended on a Conestoga village in Millersville, Pennsylvania, and murdered six Indians and burned their cabins. They burned the treaty document as well. The governor of the state, John Penn, moved immediately to protect the remaining fourteen Conestogas by placing them in protective custody in the Lancaster jail. But the Paxton Boys broke in on December 27 and massacred twelve of them, mutilating their bodies.

Every tribe had its own rituals for sending the spirits of the departed into the afterlife, but the Conestogas were a dwindling band, and no ceremonies were performed for those massacred. In ghost lore, that is a recipe for restless spirits.

Fast forward nearly one hundred years. In 1852 Christopher Hager, a Lancaster businessman, wanted to bring some class to town by establishing a theater and community building. The old jail site was selected and Hager had the jail razed, albeit reluctantly. He retained the rear foundation of the jail and had it incorporated into the new Fulton Hall. When completed, the new building was four stories high and was the largest and finest building of its kind in the entire state. Besides serving as a theater, it featured a shooting gallery on the top floor, and a storage area for stinky fertilizer and tobacco in the basement.

Famous people performed at the hall, including John Wilkes Booth, an actor regarded in his time as the most handsome man in America, who went down in infamy for assassinating President Abraham Lincoln in 1865 at Ford's Theater in Washington, D.C. Mark Twain lectured at the hall in 1872, and Buffalo Bill Cody and Wild Bill Hickock performed there in 1873.

In 1873 Fulton Hall was extensively renovated and converted into an opera house and continued to attract a stellar lineup of stars. Among them were John Phillip Sousa, Ethel Barrymore,

W.C. Fields, Sarah Bernhardt, Marie Cahill, Al Jolson, Helen Hayes, Irene Dunne, and Anna Pavlova. There were more reincarnations to come. In 1904 it was converted to a vaudeville theater, and the individual seats were replaced by pews in order to cram in more people. In the 1920s, it served as a motion picture house for "talkies," which continued through World War II.

By the 1960s, the building had deteriorated and was in danger of being demolished. A nonprofit foundation was formed in 1963 to preserve the theater, and in 1969 it was placed on the National Registry of Historic Places. It is now the oldest continually operating theater in America. Today, it is an active theater where regional performing arts groups offer a variety of productions, including musicals, dramas, ballets, and cabaret. Its restored interior evokes an earlier era with its stained glass windows, plaster columns, and wainscot of *scagolia*, an Italian faux marble technique.

The Fulton Opera House has ghosts aplenty. Ghostly sounds of applause are heard on many occasions, and an old player piano starts up by itself. The ghost of Bernhardt, who performed on stage there in 1912, is occasionally reported, and visitors sometimes glimpse an unknown female ghost wearing nineteenth-century clothing.

Phantom screams have been heard in the theater near the old original foundation of the jail, and some believe they are the ghostly voices of the Conestogas as they were massacred. In 1998, the theater brought in representatives of different tribes to perform ceremonies for the dead in hopes of setting the Conestogas' spirits to rest. The rites were performed on Water Street, where the original foundation and now the back door to the theater exist. In these ceremonies, the dead are believed to depart in winds. After the ceremony, one administrative office, which had been locked, looked as though a whirlwind had swept through, ransacking the place. Screams still linger, but perhaps they are only "imprints," a phantom record, of the horrific event.

Marie Cahill, a silent film star, appears in the opera house dressed all in white. She is most frequently noticed exiting the rear door on Water Street.

Also during the 1990s, a construction worker doing renovations was so spooked by something that he fled the theater and was apprehended by police several blocks away. He refused to say what he had seen or experienced, but he swore he would never return to the theater.

Some visitors are reluctant to go up to the "peanut gallery" on the top floor, where the shooting gallery once was located. Perhaps some of the shooting was directed at people, rather than targets, and their ghosts are still present. Television film crews and camera-toting visitors have found their cameras malfunction inside the theater.

Thomas Joseph Ambrose Ryan, a Lancaster actor who has performed at the Fulton, once saw a ghost at the theater. "In the main entrance of the lobby, I was walking with two friends," he said. "There was this white sort of mist just hovering up the stairs. When it reached the American flag pole, it just disappeared. We went the other way. It was pretty creepy." Asked if he believed in ghosts, Ryan said, "Yes, I do now."

CHAPTER 16

General Sutter Inn
LITITZ

VISITORS TO LITITZ in the Amish countryside in Lancaster County often notice the smell of chocolate. It is not a phantom haunting from the past, but the real smell of one of the important local industries, the making of chocolate and cocoa. Since 1884, the Wilbur Chocolate Company has been making chocolate—about 150 million pounds a year among its facilities in the area. The Wilbur facility is only two blocks from the General Sutter Inn. Adding to the chocolate is the aroma of freshly baked pretzels coming from the Sturgis Pretzel Bakery. No wonder Lititz is at the top of my list of haunted must-see places.

The history of the General Sutter Inn dates to the town's founding by the Moravians in 1764. Its namesake, John Augustus Sutter, a Swiss immigrant who became famous in the California Gold Rush, is buried in Lititz.

The Moravians came to America from Germany in search of utopia. They were not the only Europeans with that dream—many immigrants saw the fresh land and rich resources as the ideal place to have the perfect community, anchored in peace, harmony and cooperation, free of violence and war. In 1756, the Moravian Church was formed by John Hus. The Moravians were granted sanctuary from religious persecution.

Lititz was named after the Bohemian town of Lidice. Strict rules of living were laid down, and only persons who signed agreements to follow those rules were allowed to settle in the town. The Moravians wanted to do their best to ensure that their community would be "free from all dangerous and worldly connections, and live a peaceful and quiet life in Godliness and Honesty."

The Moravians proclaimed that in Lititz there would be no "light-minded, disorderly and needless conversation, no changing of professions, no giving a night's lodging to any person, no undertaking a journey, either far or near, without permission.... [and] no dancing, taverning, feasting at weddings, christenings or burials, common sports and pastimes and the playing of the children in the streets." The regulations warned, "They that have inclinations that way cannot live in Litiz."

The rules further stated that "parents shall be accountable for their children and families, and when any of them misbehaved or do amiss, it shall be required at their hand." In addition, all marriages were to be arranged in the following manner: the names of eligible women were put into a coconut shell, and eligible men would draw a name to select a wife. Love would come when duty was served. As for romance, there was no place for it.

Those rules seem heavy and oppressive today, but Lititz attracted settlers who were ready to give up worldly pleasures in exchange for a spiritual life of peace.

Built in 1764, the inn was initially called Zum Anker meaning "Sign of the Anchor." It was built strictly "for the necessary entertainment of strangers and travellers" passing through town, and while good food was served, no dancing, cursing, or gossip was allowed.

No matter how ideal a vision about proper behavior may be, human nature eventually prevails. People need pleasure to relieve drudgery and to make life enjoyable. By 1856 the Moravian Church was unable to police everyone's activities, and the rules were abolished. Lititz opened its doors to all religions.

John Sutter came to America from Switzerland in 1834 in order to escape creditors. He went to California, where he started a settlement near Sacramento. He became a naturalized citizen of Mexico in order to qualify for a land grant and was given eleven leagues (a league averages about three miles); he named his new place New Helvetia, or New Switzerland. The discovery of gold at his sawmill in 1849 launched the great California Gold Rush, and Sutter's land was overrun by eager prospectors. They trampled his crops, stole his horses and equipment and slaughtered his livestock for food. In 1865, a vagrant ex-soldier who had been staying at Sutter's Hock Farm burned it to the ground.

The Sutters went to Washington, D.C., to pursue reimbursement. Sutter suffered from rheumatism, and while on the East Coast they visited Lititz for the mineral springs waters there. Sutter liked the town and built a grand home across the street from the inn in 1871. Sutter died in 1880 in a hotel in Washington, D.C., while still trying to get the federal government to pay him for his ruined property. He was a Lutheran, but was given a burial anyway in the Moravian cemetery in Lititz, which officially was reserved only for members of the Moravian Church.

In 1930 the name of the inn was changed to the General Sutter Inn in honor of Sutter. Apparently, a portrait of him kept falling off the wall, and the staff thought it was a sign that Sutter was still around. Over the years, some who worked the dining rooms of the inn were certain the spirit of Sutter dropped by now and then to rearrange things, create a clatter, and stroll through the downstairs dining rooms.

When Ed Brophy bought the property in 1997, General Sutter's picture was located to the right of the dining room entrance. The employees felt it should be over the fire place, and one day they decided to move it. Suddenly, guests on the second and third floors reported that the lights had mysteriously gone out. About fifteen to twenty minutes later, the lights came back on without explanation. Some staff members observed that the lights had gone out when the portrait was taken down, and came back on when it was hanging in its new place.

Other ghostly phenomena have been noticed by the staff and guests. Once a relative of Brophy's was upstairs walking in the hallway. As she passed a room, she saw the black silhouette of a woman standing at one of the dressers. She thought it was their former housekeeper, Kitty. "Kitty, what are you doing up here so late?" she asked. But the woman turned away from her.

She again said, "Kitty, what are you doing?" The woman scurried off to the side and disappeared. Brophy's relative went back to her room and locked the door. She was so rattled by the experience that she didn't tell the story for almost a year.

One night Brophy was in the ballroom and kept hearing a terrible thumping on the ceiling. There is nothing over the ceiling but a flat roof—no attic or crawl space. He thought the noise was coming from the kitchen because of the way it reverberated through the ceiling and the wall. He went to the kitchen to tell whoever was making the noise to stop. He found no one was creating the racket. Brophy went back to reset the tables and once again heard the thumping coming from the ceiling. Again, he went back to the kitchen and asked the chef who was making the noise. The chef said no one was doing anything to make such a sound.

The next morning a husband and wife staying in Room 212 checked out. They told the employee at the front desk, "You know, we had the most incredible experience last night." The wife woke up in the middle of the night and looked towards the sink. She saw a little boy like a ghostly apparition. She woke up her husband, who got up to look, but the boy had vanished. The couple laughed about it at the front desk, thinking it spooky.

Another couple, who had stayed in Room 214, came downstairs to check out. They said they heard a terrible thumping in the middle of the night. They got up repeatedly and opened the door. As soon as they opened it, the racket stopped. They went out in the hallway, which was strangely ice cold, but saw nothing. Finally they locked the door and went back to bed.

The staff has had many other odd experiences. Apparitions of a boy and girl have been seen. Sometimes employees have come running up from the basement with the hair standing up on the backs of their necks, saying they had to get out as fast as possible because of a heavy presence. Late one night, an employee went upstairs to get towels from a linen closet and saw what appeared to be an apparition of a woman in period dress walking down the hallway. Was it the same woman seen by Brophy's relative? If so, no one knows her identity.

A former employee said one night while working there, he was near the front desk and looked up at the stairs. There was a figure of a man in uniform at the top of the stairs. He stared at it and then glanced away. When he looked back the figure was gone. Was it Sutter? The major general was known to have a fondness for his uniforms.

John and Kelly Weaver, founders of the Spirit Society of Pennsylvania, have stayed several times at the inn and have conducted investigations there. Kelly is a psychic and medium. The couple frequently travels with their dog, Teddy Bear, who is not immune to ghostly phenomena himself.

On their first visit, they stayed in Room 210. "We experienced the unnerving and unexplained movement of a tea candle on the mantle into a paper bowl we were using for Teddy's food," said John. "The flare-up singed the wallpaper. We told the front desk, who simply confirmed that 'strange things happen here.'"

On a return visit, the Weavers stayed in Room 220. John brought some of his investigation equipment and explored around the inn. He recorded EVP voices on the second and third floors. Kelly strongly sensed ghostly presences. Most unusual was Teddy Bear's behavior—something "spooked" the dog that evening and also during the night while the Weavers slept. Teddy was unusually snappish, very unlike his usual docile self. John left his recorder running all night and into the morning while the couple went downstairs to breakfast. On playback, they heard sounds of Teddy whimpering and whining as though in distress. Strange sounds of laughter were interspersed with agitated barks, and a crashing noise sounded like the dog had lunged at something. Did Teddy have invisible guests? Clearly, animals can be haunted, too!

CHAPTER 17

Alfred's Victorian Restaurant
MIDDLETOWN

DINNER WITH THE GHOSTS—many eating establishments have tried it as an entertainment theme, but no place matches the haunting ambience and great food of Alfred's Victorian Restaurant. Alfred's is Victorian to the nines, a veritable time machine to the past, and its resident ghost likes to let the customers know she is still around.

Alfred's originally was a stately Victorian home built in 1888 by Charles Raymond, who insisted on the finest luxuries. The house sits in an elegant area in Middletown, Dauphin County's oldest community, located between Lancaster and Carlisle. Middletown was an important nineteenth-century manufacturing and transportation center along the Union and Pennsylvania Canals and also along the Pennsylvania Railroad. The industrialists who thrived there displayed their wealth in their homes. The neighborhood chosen by Raymond was renowned as the most fashionable area in town.

Raymond's display of wealth eventually became his undoing, and in 1896 a bank seized his home. It changed hands several times through the years, deteriorating under the benign neglect of a series of owners. The home eventually was purchased by Alfred Pellegrini, a restaurateur of Hershey, who had a vision to restore it and open it as a fine dining establishment. Pellegrini's dream was realized in 1970. His meticulous restoration earned Alfred's a place on the National Register of Historic Places. Today diners enjoy the lush comfort of heavy burgundy and gold fabrics, brocades and draperies, plush chairs, dark woods, and intimate dining areas.

Despite the renovations, which often deteriorate haunting phenomena, Alfred's ghosts have stayed on. Perhaps they knew they would have their "old" place back.

The primary ghost of Alfred's is believed to be Emma, the second wife of Simon Cameron Young, who bought the home in 1902. Emma loved the place and died at age ninety in 1948. It is not known how long Emma has been haunting the place, but her presence became dramatic during the renovation undertaken by the Pellegrinis. Rumors that Emma committed suicide—one account says her lover jilted her, another says he died in World War I—are not true. Emma died a natural death and is buried in Middletown.

Her rocking chair rocks by itself and the scent of her favorite lavender perfume wafts through the air. Emma moves and tosses objects, and fiddles with the lights and cooking equipment.

Kelly Weaver is a popular psychic and medium who has been

coming to Alfred's since the mid-990s. Kelly and her husband John, who live in Camp Hill, are founders of the Spirit Society of Pennsylvania. They have conducted investigations at the restaurant. Kelly has a loyal clientele of Alfred's customers who like to attend the Weavers' haunted dinners there. While guests dine, John gives a talk on the history and phenomena regarding the restaurant, and Kelly gives mini-readings to each guest.

"Just about every type of paranormal activity has been witnessed at Alfred's," said Kelly. "This is clearly a classic 'intelligent' haunting."

Kelly has seen numerous examples of Emma's presence and has talked to staff over the years about them. A chef once described how Emma threw his pots and pans around, knocked on the kitchen door, and made it swing open. If he was busy, he would tell her to go bother someone else. She always obeyed.

Emma always has the last word, however, by making things in the kitchen disappear and then reappear in odd places. Once an expensive bowl of crabs vanished, only to be found in an upstairs dining room. Coffee pots have been overturned and left on the floor.

Housekeepers report cold breezes, table place settings being disturbed, and a woman's voice that calls out to them. Cleaning supplies are moved around.

Emma plays with the music selections in the restaurant, suddenly changing the easy listening and classical music to hard rock—not exactly conducive to a romantic dinner. She also will turn the music on after it has been turned off. Emma changes drink orders and makes a life-sized mannequin on the second floor move.

In the women's bathroom, Emma tosses potpourri at guests. One of the funniest incidents witnessed by the Weavers took place at the start of a haunted dinner. One of the guests, a well-dressed woman, excused herself to the ladies' room. She came stumbling back a few minutes later, her skirt askew, hair disheveled and pantyhose down around her ankles. She breathlessly told the fifty guests that she had witnessed the potpourri fly off the toilet tank and hit the door with intense force. "I'm not going back in there!" she said.

In the men's room, Emma sets off a freshener that sends fragrant puffs into the air.

Flashes of light and columns of light have been seen around the restaurant. A mysterious blue streak was captured on 35mm film in the late 1990s. The streak manifested on the landing of the main staircase. A shadowy figure was captured moving on the wall near the staircase on a camcorder in 2008.

One housekeeper had a startling experience with an apparition. Every year, Alfred's closes after Christmas for housecleaning. The housekeeper, Jeannie, was working in the parlor when she noticed a small dark silhouette from the waist up. It appeared to be a woman wearing a dark coat with an upturned collar. Jeannie thought perhaps she had come in with delivery people or was someone who needed help. The figure went into the kitchen and Jeannie followed—only to find the kitchen empty. Was it Emma?

"I feel Emma—if that is indeed her name—has a deep love for this lovely restaurant and loves the good energy brought by generations of happy customers," Kelly said.

Kelly also senses a male presence. "His demeanor suggests someone who was in banking or finance, and I suspect he may have been involved with the bank that acquired the place when Charles Raymond could not keep up with his payments." Kelly dubbed this ghost "George" and said he likes to frequent the upstairs bar and an adjacent room called the Magnolia Room.

John Weaver has encountered Emma. Once during the taping of a show for a local television station, John let people out the door. As he was closing it, he heard a female voice call out,

"Don't shut the door!"

The Weavers have organized several after-hours investigations at Alfred's and have captured EVP voices. A woman's face, believed to be Emma, was seen in a bathroom mirror. The door to the men's room has opened and closed by itself.

Activity at the restaurant is constant, and it often kicks up a few notches after the Weavers have been present. "We think Emma likes to play with Kelly, given the amount of activity reported during and after many of her events," said John. Kelly agreed that Emma seems comfortable with their presence and doesn't mind showing herself. She seems comfortable with the customers, too.

Spotlight on Ghosts:
Mirrors: Do You Know What's Looking Back At You?

Since ancient times, mirrors—or any shiny surfaces—have been regarded as portals to the unseen realms of ghosts and spirits. They can be used to summon the dead. Sometimes, in the case of hauntings, the ghosts themselves seem to use mirrors to look in on the living. Many a person staying in a haunted hotel or inn has seen a phantom face in a mirror.

What makes a mirror a portal to the afterlife? No one really knows, but conjecture holds that mirrors somehow warp or bend interdimensional space and perhaps even time itself. Whatever the process, mirrors have served up the dead for hundreds of years.

Summoning the dead in such a way typically has involved rituals of gazing into shiny surfaces to induce altered states of consciousness. Eventually ghostly images manifest and, hopefully, communicate with the living. Some people today use mirrors with black-coated backs, which minimize reflections and create shiny, inky pools ideal for the formation of ghostly faces and places. Such a mirror is called a "psychomanteum," a Greek term meaning a place where the dead are contacted. It can take a strong stomach to do such work.

Most people who see ghosts in mirrors encounter them accidentally when they visit or stay in haunted locations. Are the images real ghosts or just the imagination? Those who have experienced such images are often unable to sort out the difference.

There are numerous other folk beliefs about mirrors. In addition to showing ghosts and even the devil and demons, they also steal souls, sucking out the life force of those who gaze into them. They must be handled carefully in regard to corpses. When a person dies,

Spotlight on Ghosts:
Mirrors: Do You Know What's Looking Back At You?
(continued)

the folklore goes, all the mirrors in a house should be turned over or covered, for if a corpse sees itself in a mirror, the soul of the dead will have no rest or will become a vampire. It may become stuck in the mirror. Corpses who see themselves in mirrors also will bring bad luck upon the household. Such beliefs hark back to days when the corpses were laid out in homes, and people believed that souls lingered about the body until burial.

By the way, the notion that vampires cannot see themselves in mirrors is more fiction than folklore, thanks to Bram Stoker and his novel *Dracula*. Stoker played on the widespread belief that evil entities have no soul, and thus there is nothing to reflect in a mirror.

CHAPTER 18

Bube's Brewery and Central Hotel
MOUNT JOY

YOU CAN'T MISS BUBE'S BREWERY in tiny Mount Joy—the landmark Victorian-era building sits on a corner in brick and purple trim glory. The glory on the inside is charmingly faded, but the food and beer draw a full house of regular patrons. The establishment features intimate dining rooms, a tavern, dining in mysterious catacombs, a few hotel rooms each done in a different theme decor—and ghosts wandering about seeking to mingle with customers. There's plenty of extracurricular phantom activity to keep you coming back again and again.

Bube's has it roots in authentic German beer. The name is pronounced Boo-bee's, and is a German surname dating to sixteenth-century Europe. In the nineteenth century, Alois Bube, born in 1851, emigrated from Germany to Pennsylvania, armed with a recipe for excellent beer. Alois's primary motivation for coming to America was to dodge the draft for the Franco-Prussian War, which started in 1870. Alois landed a job at the Knapp Brewery in Lancaster. There he met Pauline, a German émigré whom he married. They settled in Mount Joy, where Alois bought the brewery and Central Hotel in 1876.

The brewery was already well established, featuring a fine Victorian dining setting, an underground of catacombs, an excellent location, and respectable beer. Alois was about to make the beer better and put the place on the map.

Alois was an Old World, old-style Bavarian brewmaster. He had a secret recipe and followed his own intuition. Every day, Alois tasted his brew and made gut-level decisions about when to move the brew from one stage of development to another. He never wrote any of it down, out of fear that someone might steal his secrets.

The beer was wildly popular, and the Central Hotel became a convenient destination on the rail line between Harrisburg and Philadelphia. Customers could get off at Mount Joy, enjoy a fine German meal and brew at Bube's, and then catch a later train. Or, if they were so inclined—and perhaps so full of food and beer—they could stay overnight in the hotel and carry on the next day.

Both Alois and Pauline had jobs at the establishment. Life was good and they had five daughters and one son. Alois was only fifty-seven when one day, in 1908, he suffered a severe heart attack and died on the spot. No one was prepared for his death. And no one could reproduce his famous brew. However, Alois had smartly saved a large sum of money, and his family was able to live on in the establishment.

In 1916, Pauline died. In 1920, Bube's closed, and Josie, one of the daughters, and her husband, Henry Engle, inherited the property. Why none of the other siblings received a share is not known. Over the next forty years, the brewery and hotel declined. Josie died in 1947, and Henry died in 1965 without a will. Their two children were sent to mental institutions for the remainders of their lives.

By 1965, the once-glorious brewery and hotel was in ruins and empty. The property was purchased by Sam Allen, the present owner, who lovingly restored it beginning in 1968. Once again, Bube's became the place to eat, drink, and be seen.

Bube's features the Alois restaurant, the original Victorian dining rooms and bar on the main floor; a larger room upstairs, and The Catacombs dining rooms, several stories downstairs. Several overnight rooms are on the third floor. The establishment's casual restaurant and tavern, The Bottling Works, is next door in the old brewery facility.

It wasn't long before staff and customers noticed that extras came along with an evening—apparitions, phantom touches, mysterious voices, music, and sounds.

Rick Fisher, the founder and president of the Paranormal Society of Pennsylvania, has devoted more time than any other paranormal investigator to collecting evidence at Bube's. He has recorded more than two hundred EVPs in various rooms there. Most of the communicators do not provide enough information to connect them to the brewery. Possibly, they were customers at one point in time—or they simply find their way in during investigations with a desire to make themselves known to the living.

The most startling communicator was a woman who said, "I wouldn't want to get you for rape." The EVP was recorded in the Peacock Room, one of the dining areas in the northeast corner on the main floor and one of the most paranormally active rooms in the establishment. The Peacock Room was used by the Bubes as a family dining room and as a parlor for entertaining friends. Rick went back to the room several times to try to reestablish contact with the communicator and obtain more information, but without success—which is often the case with EVP.

I have investigated at Bube's numerous times with Rick and other researchers and have used a Frank's Box—a device used to record EVPs in real time, using radio frequencies. On one occasion, I was downstairs on a lower level in what is called the Art Gallery—a small room with exhibits and art—with Rick and Craig Telesha. We were using a box, and recording with digital recorders and video cameras. When I asked if anyone was present who wished to communicate, a man's voice said, "Steve." I asked, "Steve, are you here?" The voice said, "I am here, I am here." Steve had no more to say than that, and we never learned who he was and why he was speaking out at Bube's.

Rick has experienced other phenomena at Bube's. Once he was on his way upstairs to the hotel rooms and said out loud for the benefit of any spirits, "Thanks for talking to me today." He was near a bathroom door that was ajar, and it closed by itself, apparently in response to him.

Rick also ran Ouija board experiments in the Peacock Room, using a man and woman to operate the board under camera and recorder surveillance. In all, he supervised twelve sessions, but only once did something peculiar happen. In the first session (at which I was present as an observer) a disembodied voice called out, "Hey!" Several persons in the room heard it. As for the board, the pointer remained inactive throughout all the sessions. Apparently the ghosts like to communicate in other ways.

Alois Bube is believed to be present, showing up as a ghostly man in period clothing. He has been seen sitting in the Peacock Room by Janet Allen, wife of owner Sam Allen. Other male ghosts have been seen walking through the building. Ghostly faces have been seen reflected in windows and mirrors.

Some of the ghosts are noisy, banging doors and china and silverware. CD players start playing music by themselves, and lights go on and off by themselves. Down in the catacombs dining rooms, the ghost of a woman in nineteenth-century garb has been seen walking around, and an invisible ghost has made sounds like place settings falling from tables to the floor—without a single piece of cutlery ever found out of place.

The catacombs are especially alluring. Dining there is like eating in an underground cavern. The catacombs were not created just for Bube's. Long before the establishment was built, catacombs, caverns, and underground springs existed beneath the town of Mount Joy. According to lore, a limestone cave near the brewery was once occupied in the eighteenth century by an eccentric known as the White Hermit. The story goes that, in his isolation, he once had a vision in which a voice ordered him to take off his clothes and go about naked—which he did. Local residents would glimpse him moving in and out of his cave in the altogether. He told others that he had done extensive exploration of the subterranean caves, chambers, and passages, and that they extended for miles. After he died, the hermit was said to haunt the area. Some believe that he uses the underground passages to access Bube's, where he is responsible for some of the haunting phenomena.

CHAPTER 19

Accomac Inn
WRIGHTSVILLE

NOT FAR FROM CODORUS FURNACE, near Wrights-
ville, is the Accomac Inn, haunted by the ghosts of an executed
murderer and his victim, as well as phantoms from the Civil
War. The Accomac Inn no longer has overnight accommoda-
tions, but it boasts one of the finest restaurants in Pennsylvania.
You can enjoy a gourmet meal and hope to spot one of the apparitions seen on the premises and grounds.

The murder that took place at the Accomac Inn in the late
nineteenth century was a tragedy of unrequited love, a true story
full of heartbreak about two young lives that ended in blood.
Prior to that, a history laced with violence brought other ghostly
residents to the place.

The land on which the inn was built on the shores of the Susquehanna River was in dispute in the early eighteenth century between Pennsylvania and Maryland. Pennsylvania eventually won, and in 1722 the tract became the first land grant west of the Susquehanna River. Ferry passengers used the site when crossing the river from the town of Marietta. In 1771, James Anderson was operating a ferry, and conveyed two hundred acres of land to his son, James Jr., described in the legal records as "innkeeper."

No one knows when the limestone inn was actually built, but it probably started as a colonial farmhouse and ferry house. It was operating as Anderson's Ferry Inn by 1775. Although a century would pass before the inn became known as the Accomac Inn, but an Accomac Road connecting the inn and the town of Hellam was known by 1750. Accomac comes from the Nanticoke Indian word "Acaumauke," meaning "across the water." It is certainly a fitting name for a ferry operation.

During the Revolutionary War, the inn was an important way station for travelers. The ferry crossing there was considered to be one of the safest. From September 30, 1777 to June 28, 1778, the Continental Congress was headquartered in York, and numerous important figures traveled back and forth across the river. Among them was the Marquis de Lafayette; Henry Laurens, the president of the Continental Congress; and colonial military officers. Lafayette recorded in a letter that one of his river crossings took place on February 3, 1778, and that the river was full of ice.

After the war, the inn changed hands several times. Its business dropped when the world's longest covered bridge—one-and-a-quarter miles in length—was built across the Susquehanna from Wrightsville to Columbia, but the ferry service and inn managed to survive. In the early 1800s, the ferry was known as Keesey's Ferry. In 1825, the first iron steamboat, named

"Codorus" after the iron furnace, was launched there.

Times were peaceful until the Civil War, when death came to the area. By 1863, Confederate troops were forcing Pennsylvanians to flee westward across the river. Union generals figured the Confederates would try to capture a bridge, but placed their bets on the state's capital, Harrisburg. While Union troops were concentrated there, the Confederates staged an attack on the Wrightsville bridge on June 28, 1863. After ninety minutes of intense shelling, the Union forces retreated, setting fire to the bridge as they went. The bridge burned completely, preventing the Confederates from crossing the river. A few days later, the tide turned against the South at the Battle of Gettysburg.

An unknown Confederate soldier is buried alongside the road near the inn. No one knows who he is, or how he died. Several stories have circulated over the years. One holds that he died of illness at the inn and was buried there. Another says that he was a spy who drowned trying to swim across the river, and his body washed ashore there. Still another story holds that he was a scout and got caught in a storm and died.

The burning of the bridge benefited the ferry service, and business picked up. In 1864, John Coyle purchased the inn and the final tragic chapter of its history began. Coyle changed the name of the inn to Accomac around 1875. He and his wife, Mary, had a son, also named John. The boy was described as having a "weak mind," which means he may have been mentally ill. He grew up to become a riverman—and a heavy drinker.

Mary developed painful and crippling arthritis, and in the early 1880s John hired a teenaged girl, Emily Myers, to live with them and take care of her. Emily was an orphan who lived in Marietta. She was happy to be invited to be part of a family and accepted the job. Descriptions of her say she was beautiful, with dark hair and mysterious gray eyes. She was hard-working, but not very bright.

Johnny fell head over heels in love with Emily, but she spurned his advances. He persisted, proposing marriage to her several times. Every rejection made him more determined to have her. His frustration escalated into anger.

On the morning of May 30, 1882, Johnny decided to take drastic action. He armed himself with a gun and went to the barn where Emily was milking cows. He proposed again, and once again she turned him down. Johnny drew out his gun and threatened to shoot her if she refused him again. She did. As she turned away from him, she said, "Johnny, I am never going to marry any man."

Those were Emily's last words. Johnny fired his gun. The bullet penetrated her body, killing her almost instantly.

Horrified at what he had done, Johnny fled into the woods. He eluded capture for ten days. He was charged with first-degree murder, and he was to stand trial in York. Johnny pled not guilty on the grounds of insanity on the advice of his attorneys. After a sensational trial, he was found guilty. The case was appealed to the Pennsylvania Supreme Court and Johnny was granted a retrial. His attorneys had the venue changed to Gettysburg, hoping for a more sympathetic treatment. But there was no mercy for Johnny there either. A jury quickly found him guilty of first-degree murder on March 5, 1883. Several more attempts at appeals failed. Johnny was sentenced to die by hanging.

Several days before he was scheduled to be executed, a team of physicians from Philadelphia examined him and pronounced him insane. This did not sway the governor, who declared that Johnny must die, insane or not.

The end for Johnny came on April 22, 1884 in Gettysburg. He had a final meal of Susquehanna shad steak, bread and butter, and coffee. His grief-stricken parents paid their final visit, leaving him at 10:30 in the morning. *The York Gazette* reported the sorrowful scene in detail, describing "the hot tears of deep grief and distress rolling fast and thick down over their wrinkled cheeks."

Three hundred people watched as he was led to a gallows, hooded, and then hanged. After twenty minutes of twitching, Johnny went into the afterlife. He was pronounced dead at 11:25 A.M.

His heartbroken mother took his body home and had him buried fifty feet south of the inn. His gravestone reads:

My Son
John D. Coyle
Born
March 15, 1855
Died
April 22, 1884
Aged 29 years, 1 month and 7 days
"Mother dear,
weep not for I am not dead
but sleeping here."

The Coyles were never the same, and in 1889 they sold the inn to James Duffy. The inn passed through various owners. It flourished as an upscale establishment, touting its menu—chicken and waffles dinners were a specialty—and its social events. After the development of the automobile, it prospered even more, for its patrons could drive to it, eat, and go home the same day.

"Ye Old Accomac Inn" was well settled into genteel prosperity when once again violence visited, this time in the form of fire. The inn was destroyed on May 16, 1935. A neighbor noticed the flames and roused the owners, Norman Pickle and his wife. The couple escaped with only the clothes they were wearing, and watched helplessly while the fire consumed everything, right down to the foundation.

Pickle immediately began reconstruction, using some of the original stone that survived the fire, plus new stone from the Witmer Bridge. Reconstruction went quickly, and the inn reopened on September 21 the same year. The new three-story structure was as close to the original as possible.

The inn reestablished itself, regaining its popularity. The present owner, H. Douglas Campbell Jr., purchased the property in 1971.

Some blame the fire on the ghosts of Johnny and Emily, restless in their tragedies. Before the inn burned, the barn where Emily had milked the cows burned down. How did the two fires start? Can ghosts cause a blaze?

Reconstruction and renovation sometimes bring an end to hauntings, but not at the Accomac. Once the inn was back in business, employees noticed odd things happening. Dishes set on tables at night were found smashed on the floor in the morning. Objects were moved about. Sounds of music and a woman's voice floated in the air. Employees felt watched by invisible presences. Doors opened and closed by themselves. A ghostly man appeared sitting in the bar. Was it Johnny, who loved his liquor?

A ghost of a young woman believed to be Emily was seen once sitting outside the inn on a step. She was dressed in period clothing and was weeping. A witness offered her help, thinking she was a living person. She waved the witness away, and when he returned to try to help again, she had vanished. Staff have seen the ghosts of a young man and woman inside the inn.

Other phenomena reported at the inn are sensations of being watched, odd flashes seen in mirrors, and whistling and voices coming from empty rooms. Johnny's ghost is said to even visit nearby residents, where he rearranges furniture and speaks in a muffled voice.

The second floor, which would have been where overnight guests stayed long ago, is the most active. Now it holds dining rooms. A female voice has been heard in empty areas, and a presence has been sensed in the ladies' restroom.

Johnny's tombstone near the inn can still be visited, as well as the grave of the unknown Confederate soldier, located about one-half mile down the road by the riverside.

Spotlight on Ghosts: Rethinking Orbs

Those fuzzy round dots floating in digital photographs are not spirits or ghosts—or are they? Most paranormal investigators dismiss orbs, but some are calling for a re-examination of them. Maybe cameras are capturing some unknown life force after all.

Prior to digital photography, orbs were uncommon in photos. Usually not seen with the naked eye, they showed up mysteriously in hard prints. Digital cameras record them frequently, and many people interpret every fuzzy blotch on a photo as a ghost or spirit—much to the chagrin of photographic experts.

According to paranormal investigators, the overwhelming majority of orbs can be explained, even debunked, as natural effects of digital equipment or atmospheric conditions. Dust, moisture, and insects—especially those close to the camera lens—can come out looking like mysterious blobs of semitransparent light.

Still, even the harshest skeptics acknowledge that a tiny percentage of orb photos cannot be explained. Perhaps it is true what orb enthusiasts say: our improved photographic technology enables us to capture evidence of life forms that are, for the most part, below the register of human perception.

Some orb enthusiasts hold that they can deliberately attract orbs and cause them to show up in their photographs, thus arguing that an unknown, responsive intelligence is at work. Indeed, some orb photographs are hard to explain away as particles in the air.

Physicist William A. Tiller, who has applied science to the study of intention and its impact on the physical environment, says that the recent, prolific appearance of orbs is not accidental, but is the first sign of an unfolding of "communications manifestations." Tiller

Spotlight on Ghosts:
Rethinking Orbs
(continued)

holds that humans can condition an environment to attract orbs and increase their responsiveness to thought, emotion, and intention. If so, more researchers should turn their attention to the mystery of the orb.

Nonetheless, examine all possible natural explanations when looking at orb photos. Many haunted locations have dusty floors, and when dust is kicked into the air it will show up in your photographs.

CHAPTER 20

Chickie's Rock
LANCASTER COUNTY

VISIT CHICKIE'S ROCK on the Susquehanna River between Columbia and Marietta day or night and be prepared for a supernatural smorgasbord of phenomena. This two-hundred-foot-high chunk of quartzite teems with ghosts, mysterious creatures who like to steal apples, shadowy figures, and phantom voices and sounds.

Chickie's was originally spelled "Chiques," from the Susquehannock name "Chiquesalunga," which means "place of the crayfish." Chiquesalunga is the name of a nearby creek. Chickie's Rock looms over a bend in the Susquehanna, the star attraction in a 422-acre regional park named, appropriately, Chickie's Rock Park. Breath-taking views can be seen up and down the river.

Many of the ghosts are tied to the site's colorful history. White settlers moved in on Native Americans in the 1700s and 1800s and set up iron furnaces on a canal that ran alongside the river. The village of Chickies at the base of the rock thrived until the early 1900s, when the iron industry began a move westward and a railroad line replaced dependency on the canal. The iron furnaces shut down one by one, and soon the entire village was abandoned. Today the crumbling ruins of houses and taverns in this ghost town are covered with vegetation.

Lancaster County established the park in 1977. Hiking trails afford easy access to the spectacular overlooks and also wind around the base and along the village ruins. The rock itself is popular with rock climbers. A wood rail fence affords some protection at the lookouts. When you visit there, do not climb over them and risk slipping off the rock. Daredevils and thrill seekers have plummeted to their deaths that way.

Chickie's Rock has always had a supernatural air to it. Even the Indians back in colonial days talked of ghosts wandering around the rock. According to legend, star-crossed lovers met their doom there. Different versions of the story are told. In one, a nameless Indian maiden was pursued by other Indians. She reached the edge of the rock, and rather than be captured, she jumped to her death. Another version resembles the story of Romeo and Juliet, members of warring families but desperately in love with each other. The Indian brave and maiden were forbidden to see each other. One night they sneaked away to the top of the rock and made a suicide pact, believing it was better to be together in eternity than separated in life.

The most detailed legend tells of Wanunga, a Susquehannock brave who fell in love with the maiden Wanhuita. One night he took her to the rock to boast of his victories in battle and profess his love for her. Wanunga got a raw shock, for Wanhuita rejected him, confessing that she was deeply in love with a white man, one of the settlers in the village at the base of the rock.

Wanunga attacked her in a rage. Wanhuita's white lover heard her screams and dashed to her rescue. He fought Wanunga, but the brave was the stronger of the two, and he fatally slit the white man's throat. Then he grabbed Wanhuita and leaped off the rock, sending both of them to their deaths. According to lore, Wanhuita could be heard screaming "Chickie's! Chickie's!" all the way down—ghostly screams that still echo in the ethers today.

The white settlers at Chickie's were well acquainted with ghostly inhabitants. In 1875, a railroad worker reported repeatedly seeing the ghost of a man near the tracks by the tunnel. The ghost appeared between midnight and 1:00 A.M. He looked life-like, with a full beard, and he carried a staff with a red flag tied to it. Other ghosts drifting along the old railroad tracks have been seen into present times.

A legend holds that the land is not inhabitable because of a witch's curse. Before the turn of the nineteenth century, a woman who was said to be a witch lived near the rock. She lost her property due to eminent domain, and in a rage cursed the place. She is said to have used a spell from The Seventh Book of Moses, one of two German magical books of spell casting brought to America by immigrants. The Sixth and Seventh Books of Moses were rumored to be extremely powerful. According to lore, they cannot be destroyed, not even by burning, unless they are cast into a fire by a boy born on a Sunday during church sermon time.

In the early 1800s, a ferry service operated on the Susquehanna. According to lore, it was once run by a man and his son. One morning the ferry had an accident and the son was thrown into the water and drowned. His father tried in vain to recover the body, which became trapped by rocks below the water's surface. He resolved to dynamite the rocks. Supposedly the explosion tossed him into the water, and he suffered fatal injuries, dying a few days later. His ghost still wanders the shore, where he is looking for the body of his lost son.

In more recent times, the ghosts of other victims are glimpsed at the rock. Every year, people fall to their deaths or sustain serious injury while hiking too close to the edge or seeking a thrill by climbing over the fence. People have committed suicide by jumping off Chickie's. There are even stories of alleged murders committed there.

One of the most famous ghosts of Chickie's is a hoax. "Chickie's Apparition" was made up by wine-drinking teens in August 1969 as a joke on their friends. They claimed to see a gray or silver mist floating above the trees, causing people to run in fright. The story got retold and retold, and, like urban legends, took hold as "fact."

Hoax or no, however, people began reporting seeing the apparition! The mist was described as gray, green, and silver. Some people swore they saw a ghostly house appear and disappear. The stories prompted crowds of curious ghosthunters to gather at the rock at night, and police sometimes had difficulty controlling the place. Even after the teens confessed to their hoax, people still believed they saw the apparition. One self-appointed exorcist arrived with a Bible, claiming he could make ghosts appear or disappear by reading certain verses.

Eventually the fad died down, but the stories still linger in

Chickie's lore. All the publicity did inspire a woman to make public her own very real ghost encounter, which took place in 1946 when she was eighteen. The woman said that late one night, she and her colleagues from Wyeth Laboratories in Marietta went to the rock for a nighttime picnic. She and several others went to fetch water from the pump. On their way back to their site, a horrible apparition of a grotesque human-like figure leaning against a tree terrified them. It was dressed in black and about sixteen feet tall and a foot-and-a-half wide. It had no arms or feet, a mummified head, and knives sticking out if it. They fled.

The woman's parents failed to believe her story, saying it was all in her imagination in a spooky place at night. But some young men believed her and went to check it out for themselves. They claimed they, too, saw the horrible figure, and they said it moved about from one spot to another instantly, causing trees to bend as if by wind, and the ground to shake. Subsequently, other people reported seeing the figure.

Another creepy figure is a shadow person, the dark silhouetted figure of a tall man wearing a fedora-style hat and flowing cape, who walks about the woods near the top of the rock. The figure was seen at close range on October 31, 2004, by a man in a search party looking for a young man believed to be suicidal. The night was foggy and the rock was shrouded in mist, making the setting all the more eerie. Suddenly the shadow figure loomed out of the mist. It moved quickly over the ground without the appearance of feet. It wore a large-brimmed hat. Its long cloak flowed behind it as it moved swiftly through the woods and vanished. Sadly, the body of the young man was found that night.

The dark figure is not the Grim Reaper. Hatted and caped silhouette specters of tall men exist in Indian lore around America, even on the West Coast. They seem to be fond of remote areas and are usually seen standing atop cliffs and hills, where they act like sentries or watchmen. Who are they, and what are they doing? No one knows.

Perhaps most peculiar of all the mysterious inhabitants of Chickie's are the "Albatwitches," ape-like creatures four to five feet tall who live in the trees and attack picnickers in order to steal their apples. The creatures were originally called "apple snitchers," and the name morphed over time to "Albatwitches."

Rick Fisher, founder of the Paranormal Society of Pennsylvania, has investigated Chickie's Rock for years. In February 2002, Rick had a spooky experience seeing a weird creature that may have been an Albatwitch.

One morning about six, he was driving west on Route 23 toward Marietta. It was still dark, and at that hour, the road was lonely. As he neared Kinderhook Road, about two miles from Chickie's Rock, the figure of what appeared to be a man in dark clothing walking in the middle of the road loomed into his headlights. Rick slowed down, and as he got closer, he saw that the figure was smaller, about the size of a child. "What is a kid doing in the middle of the road by himself at this hour?" he wondered to himself. Then he saw the figure clearly, and a chill shot through him. The figure was no child—it was not even human! It was about five feet tall, thin as a stick, and completely covered in hair. It kept ambling down the road, apparently oblivious to Rick following it in his car. He drove slowly behind it, trying to figure out what it was. He turned on his high beams. The figure turned around, and Rick saw two yellow eyes looking him over. Abruptly, the figure vanished. Shaken, Rick pulled over to the side and sat for a while, composing himself. Then he got out and looked around in the woods to see if there was any sign of the creature. He found nothing.

Rick returned again to the same spot at the same time in the morning, but never again saw the hairy stick creature. Was it an Albatwitch?

Later, Rick heard reports of similar figures. One came from a man who had seen one on Pinkerton Road near a golf course. Another report came from a young man in Indiana. UFO and Bigfoot researcher Stan Gordon told Rick that he had collected reports of similar sightings. The mystery of who or what they are continues.

There is much more to the haunting of Chickie's Rock. Ghostly drumming has been heard by hikers, believed to be the sounds of Indian drums beaten long ago. A disembodied, cackling laugh is said to be a phantom outlaw who hid treasure near the rock. Sentenced to hang, the outlaw refused to disclose the location of the treasure, and his ghost and other spirits still guard it today.

Chickie's Rock is an EVP heaven for investigators. Rick Fisher has collected hundreds of EVPs of ghostly voices there, some of which he thinks are the victims of deadly falls.

Even if you don't see a ghost, Chickie's Rock makes a spectacular outing in any kind of weather. Just don't get too close to the edge!

CHAPTER 21

Codorus Furnace
YORK COUNTY

A **WHITE LADY GHOST,** mysterious voices, and the remnants of a legendary secret crime haunt the spooky setting of Codorus Furnace, the ruins of one of the oldest iron smelters in America. The furnace has a pedigree of prominent roles in the Revolutionary War and the War of 1812 as well as links to a signer of the Declaration of Independence.

Codorus was built in 1765 by William Bennett on a 150-acre tract of land he acquired from the William Penn family. It was originally known as Hellam Forge or Hellam Iron Works. The tower and surrounding ruins are on the south side of Codorus Creek, near the Susquehanna River. Today a two-lane road cuts the ground between the creek and the furnace. The growth of brush and trees is thick around the ruins. Drive too fast along Furnace Road, and you can pass this intriguing haunted site without ever knowing it.

The quiet wooded setting along the lush creek has a mysterious pull. "Codorus is like a magnet to me," said Melissa Telesha, of Mechanicsburg, a paranormal investigator and activities coordinator for the Spirit Society of Pennsylvania. "It is isolated and beautiful. When it gets dark, the place is completely eerie. It's lonely and frightening as soon as the sun goes down."

Iron-making was one of the first industries in the area in colonial times, and by the early 1800s there were about 170 iron ore mines in York County alone. The massive Cordorus tower was built against the side of a hill, and was constructed of stone reinforced with iron hoops. The inside was lined with sandstone and fire clay. Pig iron was made by pouring layers of iron ore, limestone, and charcoal into the furnace and melted down with blasts of hot air. The resulting molten pig iron was poured into molds. When cooled, blacksmiths worked it to make various items, such as weapons, munitions, and tools.

Despite the prosperity of the iron industry, Codorus seemed more of a curse than a blessing for its owners. Bennett went bankrupt in 1771 and the furnace passed into receivership. Charles Hamilton bought it from the sheriff, and then sold it to James Smith, a local lawyer who made history by signing the Declaration of Independence and becoming a member of the Continental Congress. Smith owned multiple iron-making operations. When the Revolutionary War began, Codorus was dedicated to the manufacture of iron for cannons, cannon balls, munitions, and pots and pans. It played a key role in rearming George Washington's troops during their winter layover at Valley Forge in 1778-79.

By then, Smith had somehow managed to lose twenty-five thousand dollars operating Codorus, and he, too, was forced into bankruptcy. He sold the furnace in 1778. It passed through a succession of owners, including a man named Thomas Neill. In 1802, Neill sold it to Henry Bates Grubb, a York businessman. Grubb enlarged the works and renamed it Codorus. The furnace supplied munitions for the War of 1812.

In 1818, Grubb hired a manager, John Shippen, who worked there until 1825. Grubb died in 1823, and his two sons, Edward and Clement, ran the furnace. Operations ceased in the 1850s, and the tower and a small house behind it on the hill fell into ruin.

The furnace and land were purchased by the Conservation Society of York County in 1949. Since then, the furnace has been restored three times, the last time in 1983. The Codorus Furnace is listed on the National Register of Historic Places and is the oldest remaining landmark of the iron industry in York County.

I have visited Codorus twice with Melissa and her husband, Craig Telesha, also a paranormal investigator, and have been similarly mesmerized by the enchanted atmosphere there, especially at dusk into darkness. Even the traffic going by on the road does not spoil the feel.

Visitors have reported seeing a white lady ghost either coming down the road from the former furnace house, where the iron masters once lived, or moving through the brush behind the furnace. Although we have yet to see her, we have recorded interesting EVP.

Once Melissa was at Codorus with two other investigators, Deb Snyder and Laura Shank. They put their digital recorders out and asked, "Is anyone here?" A male voice answered, "Thomas." Later they learned that one of the previous owners was Thomas

Neill. Returning to the site, they asked, "Is Thomas Neill here?" A male voice responded, "Yes."

No one knows the identity of the white lady or why she haunts Codorus. Legend has it that one of the iron masters had a young and beautiful mistress. She became pregnant, and he murdered her.

There is no known historical record to document that, but the story ties in with other lore concerning one of the last iron masters, a man named Trego. He lived up the road in the furnace house with his wife. Trego was a stern and sometimes cruel man, according to lore. The workers had to come to his kitchen window to get their pay, handed out by Trego's wife. If they were drunk or disorderly, he threw them into a barred cell in his basement.

A story holds that the house was restored in the 1980s, and a human skull was found beneath the floorboards. Who is it? A disciplined worker? A mistress? No one knows, and there is no known historical record of the find, but the skull story intensifies the mystery surrounding Codorus.

Members of the North Codorus Paranormal Society in Spring Grove are among those who also have investigated the site. They have gotten EVP that might shed light on the identity of the white lady. They asked, "Are you the wife of the iron master?" A female voice whispered "Yes." However, no names were given, either of the wife or her iron master husband.

Regardless of whether any crimes were committed at Codorus, one thing is certain: the place brimmed with passion in its heyday. All kinds of passion. The Colonial rebels were passionate about winning the war, and that emotional intensity went into their work at the furnace. There surely was romantic passion, whether illicit or marital. There also was the passion that is poured into industry and into building a nation.

"When I'm there, I feel the passion of a lot of people," said Melissa Telesha. "I think they left something of themselves behind. You always have the feeling that there is someone watching you."

CHAPTER 22

The Railroad House
MARIETTA

THE RAILROAD HOUSE is a charming hotel with a Southern feel in the little Susquehanna River town of Marietta. The entire town of Marietta boasts many ghosts, and the Railroad House has plenty to offer. Like the atmosphere of the inn and the staff there, the ghosts are warm and friendly, and they often like to make themselves known.

Marietta is actually a hybrid town, a combination of two towns developed side by side in 1803 and 1804 by David Cook and James Anderson. Eight years later, they saw the advantage of combining forces, and joined the two communities. They named it Marietta, after their wives Mary and Henrietta.

Marietta boomed as a river and canal town for lumbering and transportation. There was a great need for lodging and meals. The Railroad House was built between 1820 and 1823 to serve those needs. The hotel was built directly in front of the Pennsylvania Main Line Canal which ran from Philadelphia to Pittsburgh by way of the Portage Railroad.

Rivermen—renowned for their love of alcohol and fighting—frequented the hotel. One early description says that the "walls reverberated with inebriate good cheer, an occasional brawl, and all the violence and immorality of the roughest classes."

The Railroad House was able to weather the transition from boat to railroad. When the railroad, later known as the Pennsylvania Standard, replaced the canal, part of the Railroad House was converted into a waiting room and ticket office. It remained this way until 1860 when the Marietta Station was constructed across the street.

In the late 1890s, the Railroad House was operated by Colonel Thomas Scott, who had served as assistant secretary of war for President Abraham Lincoln. Scott also was a president of the Pennsylvania Railroad.

The Railroad House prospered until the 1930s and then went into decline. It survived floods and squatters, but eventually, it was sold at auction in the late 1950s. Restoration of the building began in the 1960s, and it was turned into a psychedelic coffee house. In the 1970s it was a disco. It then became a popular gourmet restaurant and tavern. In the 1980s the business was expanded to include a bed-and-breakfast with eight rooms available. Much of the early grandeur was restored.

The hotel has changed hands several times since reopening for business. In 2008, more renovations were undertaken to make the place more informal. The dining room known as the "music room" was turned into a tavern. The Front Street entrance was reopened, the vestibule and tavern floors were refinished and the walls were painted to create a casual pub atmosphere.

Ghosts are active on all floors of the Railroad House, as well as on the grounds. Many times they are heard or sensed rather than seen. In the upstairs guest quarters, Rooms 6 and 9 are particularly active.

The sound of a gunshot has been heard in Room 6; there is a story that a man committed suicide there at an unknown time by shooting himself. Guests have also heard strange knockings in the walls. One employee who stayed in the room said she felt an invisible presence get into bed with her. The feeling she had was that she was taking up all the room in the bed, and the visitor objected. She moved over and the sense of the presence went away.

In Room 9, guests are visited by a male presence that stands at the foot of the bed. Some believe it is the ghost of Colonel Scott, who lived in the room while he operated the hotel. The ghost departs if ordered to do so, but not without making a loud thumping sound. Some guests hear footsteps approaching the bed but cannot see anything. Others have had the bedclothes pulled off of them.

Other phenomena experienced throughout the hotel include the sounds of phantom typing, doors opening by themselves, the sensation of being watched by an unknown and unseen presence, door knobs rattling in the night, pushes from unseen hands, strange balls of light flying around, and an invisible dog that barks and makes clicking sounds as he walks on the hardwood floors.

The ghost of an unknown little girl, dressed in nineteenth-century clothing, has been seen in a mirror over the bar and on the stairs leading to the second floor.

In the yard behind the hotel is a cottage, once the site of the summer kitchen. Today it is guest quarters, and also houses a refrigerator, a television, and a ghost. Guests have seen the figure of an elderly woman sitting in the cottage rocking chair, knitting. Only female guests see her. When witnessed in the night, the figure will disappear if women try to wake their male companions to see her.

The garden at the Railroad House is tended by a ghost named Anne Marie. Back in the heyday of the hotel, Anne Marie would tend the garden, growing food for the kitchen. She would be friendly to all the men passing by, hoping that a rich man would notice her and want to marry her. The story goes that she died without that wish being fulfilled; perhaps that is why her ghost remains there today. She appears primarily to male staff members and to single men who sit in the beer garden, which is set up outside in warm weather.

Spotlight on Ghosts: The Ghost Dogs of Colebrook Furnace

You're driving along a lonely country road late at night. Suddenly, a large animal lunges out from the side of the road straight in front of you. There's no way to avoid hitting it. You slam on the brakes and watch it go under the wheels with a sickening thud. You stop, or look back in the rearview mirror —to find nothing.

You just had an encounter with a ghost dog.

Spectral dogs are found in folklore everywhere, and they roam the Pennsylvania countryside, too. Where they really come from nobody knows. They like to lurk along country roads, in graveyards, and in remote areas. They seem fond of running in front of vehicles only to disappear into thin air, as though they like to trick people. They terrorize others by chasing them.

Sometimes there is no story or legend to explain why ghost dogs haunt certain areas. In other cases, they are said to be the ghosts or pets or working dogs, some of whom linger out of emotional attachment. Some haunt regions because of violence and injustice.

The ghost dogs of Colebrook Furnace near Colebrook in Lebanon County met a violent and unhappy end. The furnace operated from 1791 to 1858. Pennsylvania was once full of furnaces feeding the mighty iron industry, and in those days, they were run by iron masters whose word was law.

According to legend, the Colebrook Furnace had a cruel iron master who had a pack of seventeen foxhounds. The leader of the pack was Flora, the most loyal and intelligent of the bunch. Once, she even saved the iron master's life when he got drunk and passed out in the snow. She barked to awaken servants, who discovered him and carried him inside.

One night, the iron master got drunk again and bet other men on the quality of his hounds. The next morning, he summoned them to a hunt, but strangely, the dogs would not respond. Perhaps they knew something bad was afoot. Only Flora came, and the iron master was so displeased that he whipped her mercilessly. He then declared that his dogs would hunt, or they would hunt in Hades.

Finally, the other dogs roused, and the hunt began. But no fox appeared, which further enraged the iron master. He rounded them up and went home. There he threw them into the fiery furnace one by one.

Horrified employees could hear the hounds yelping in agony in their final moments. The last to be sacrificed to the flames was Flora.

The iron master was never the same after that. He drank heavily and his health deteriorated. He kept staring at his feet, as though at an invisible dog. He took to his bed, which became his deathbed. One day he screamed out that the dogs were coming for him, and he died.

Flora and her pack of foxhounds still roam the Lebanon County countryside, howling and baying at night, protesting the injustice meted out to them.

CHAPTER 23

The Grave of Mad Anthony Wayne

WAYNE

WHO IS THE MOST FREQUENTLY SIGHTED ghost on America's east coast? Not George Washington. Not Abraham Lincoln. It is Major General Anthony Wayne, the flamboyant Revolutionary War hero. A native of Pennsylvania, he was renowned as "Mad Anthony" for his risk-taking and daring feats. He was a brilliant strategist and fought with an unrivaled intensity and fierceness. Perhaps it was his bravado that made him so feared and sealed his presence in the twilight realm of ghosts.

Or perhaps his ghost is restless because his remains have not lain peacefully in the ground.

The ghost of Wayne, sometimes with his favorite horse, Nab, is seen in several states, from Virginia to New York, constantly reenacting scenes from his glory days. His ghost also rises up from his grave in Wayne in Radnor Township, a macabre tale of its own.

Wayne was born on January 1, 1745, near Paoli in Chester County. He received an excellent education and worked as a surveyor for Benjamin Franklin. When the Revolutionary War began, he assembled a militia and became colonel of the 4th Regiment in Pennsylvania. He aided Benedict Arnold and saved General George Washington's troops from a massacre at the Battle of Brandywine in September 1777.

Wayne was at Valley Forge during the winter of 1777-78, where the Continental Army recouped and rested. When fighting resumed, Wayne led men to more victories, including a decisive battle at Stony Point along the Hudson River.

After the Revolutionary War came to a close, Wayne turned to battles with Indians. In 1796, he was traveling from a military post in Detroit to Pennsylvania. He was severely ill with gout and was in agony with stomach pains. On November 19, he arrived by boat at Presque Isle, now Erie, Pennsylvania. Wayne was whisked to the quarters of the commander of the military fort, Captain Russell Bissell, who summoned Dr. J.C. Wallace to come at once from Pittsburgh. Until Wallace could arrive, Wayne was attended by Dr. George Balfour, who doubted the general would be able to survive.

After several weeks of intense pain and discomfort, Wayne, 51, expired on December 15 in the arms of Balfour. Wallace had not yet arrived. In accordance with his wishes, Wayne, wearing his uniform, was buried two days after his death in a plain wooden coffin at the foot of the flagstaff of the post's block-house. The top of the coffin bore his initials, age, and the year of his death in brass tacks.

For twelve years, the remains of Wayne remained undis-turbed in a plain grave. Despite his wishes, some thought his burial was not fitting for so great a hero. In the fall of 1808, his thirty-eight-year-old daughter, Margaretta, fell seriously ill and was suddenly seized with the desire to have her father's body dug up and moved to the family burial plot in Radnor Township, not far from Valley Forge. Moving corpses was not uncommon in those days, but Wayne's son, thirty-seven-year-old Isaac, was against it. Margaretta convinced Isaac to do the job. He enlisted the help of Dr. Wallace, who had not arrived in time to treat Wayne during his last days.

By this time, the remains of Wayne were expected to be noth-ing more than bones, which Isaac would take in a small trunk across the state to Radnor Township by sulky, a two-wheeled horse-drawn cart. Isaac refused to attend the disinterment him-self, preferring to keep his memories of his father during life intact.

When the coffin was opened in Erie, spectators were shocked. Expecting to see crumbling bones, they saw, instead, that Wayne's body had not decomposed, except that one leg and one foot were partially gone. The rest of the body was in a remarkable state of preservation.

In Eastern Europe, this would have marked Wayne as a vampire and his corpse would have been staked or mutilated to prevent him from walking among the living. Wayne's body was mutilated, but for different and more practical reasons.

It was clear that the sulky transport was no longer adequate. It had room for a box of bones, but not a full-sized coffin con-taining a corpse. Dr. Wallace proposed an Indian solution. He dismembered the corpse and boiled the pieces in a large kettle. Working with four assistants, Wallace took a knife and whittled off the cooking flesh until the bones were clean.

Some of the observers could not help but take a few souvenirs from the great hero. The wife of Captain Dobbins, who was stationed at the fort, pulled a lock of Wayne's hair out of his head. She later wrote that the corpse was not firm, but soft like chalk. Another witness, Henry Whitney, wrote that Wayne's back flesh was four inches thick and was "firm like pork."

The boot on the decomposed foot had rotted , but Wayne's other boot was in good condition. Another witness, James Duncan, tried it on and found it to be a good fit. Quality leather boots were expensive, and Duncan saw a way to get a pair cheap. He took Wayne's boot to a shoemaker and had a mate made to match. He wore the pair until they fell apart.

Isaac was greatly distressed by this turn of events, and for the rest of his life regretted his decision to disinter his father. But once the body had been dug up, there was nothing he could do but carry on. After boiling, the bones were packed in a trunk as planned, and off they went to their new burial at St. David's Episcopal church in what is now called Wayne. The bones were interred near the old church, built in 1715 (and still close to its original condition).

The Pennsylvania State Society of the Cincinnati raised five hundred dollars for a pillar monument on the grave. Wayne finally received the grand burial ceremony that many thought he deserved. A huge crowd gathered, and the funeral procession of troops was a mile long. Isaac Wayne and other members of the family attended. An oration was delivered by Reverend David Jones, who served with Wayne during the Revolutionary War.

The kettle and tools used in the boiling were buried in Wayne's coffin in his original grave at Erie. A few decades later, the grave met with misfortune. By 1853, the old blockhouse was abandoned. On November 10, 1853, arsonists set it on fire and it burned to the ground. The parade ground was leveled off and the grave site was lost. Around 1878 a Dr. Germer of Erie found the grave and had it reopened a second time. Most of the original coffin had rotted, but the lid with its brass tacks was still intact. In 1880 the State of Pennsylvania rebuilt the blockhouse as a memorial to Anthony Wayne. It was been rebuilt several times, the last time was in 1984. The original coffin lid, some remnants of clothing, and Dr. Wallace's equipment were put on display at the rebuilt fort. The kettle mysteriously disappeared. A replica with fake bones was put on display by the Erie County History Center.

Did all of Wayne's bones make it to his new grave? According to legend, some of them did not, and so created a haunting. There are two versions to the legend. According to one, the trunk fell off the sulky and broke open several times, spilling the bones, and not all of them were recovered. According to the second version, the distressed Isaac was in a hurry and didn't notice when some of the bones fell out of the trunk. On New Year's Day—Wayne's birthday—his ghost rises from his Wayne grave and rides a horse to his old grave in Erie in search of his missing bones.

Mad Anthony's ghost also has been seen throughout Pennsylvania, and in New Jersey, New York, Canada, and as far south as Virginia. In Pennsylvania, he is seen along Route 1 near Chadd's Ford, where the battle of Brandywine was fought, and also up and down Route 30. Sometimes he is astride Nab, who has a formidable ghostly presence of fire-flashing hoofs. Whether alone or on horseback, Wayne's ghost looks fierce and determined, as though he is still waging battles against the British and Germans. Wayne's ghost also has been reported at Valley Forge National Park.

Surprisingly, Wayne's ghost was never reported at the former General Wayne Inn in Merion Station near Philadelphia. The 1704 tavern and inn was renamed after Wayne in 1793. It had Revolutionary War ghosts aplenty, but not Wayne himself. The inn is now a private establishment, the Chabad Center for Jewish Life.

Spotlight on Ghosts:
Valley Forge

In the winter of 1777–78, General George Washington encamped his beleaguered Continental Army at Valley Forge. It was a harsh winter, the troops were worn out, and the Revolutionary War was going badly for the colonialists. Washington and his top officers worked hard to revise their strategies for the coming battles of the spring.

Valley Forge is a now a national historical park, a huge sprawling place of thirty-six hundred acres that showcases how the enlisted men and officers lived. No battles were fought here, though two thousand men became ill and died. Some of them died on the grounds and some in hospitals in surrounding towns. For certain there were tense emotions, often the stuff of hauntings. But perhaps because of the lack of acute suffering and violence, Valley Forge is only mildly haunted today.

The National Park Service has the official line of "no ghosts here," which is often the case at battlefields that are obviously haunted. Privately, staff and reenacters who have spent many years at Valley Forge attest to a few ghostly remnants.

The troops were trained and exercised on the rolling farm fields temporarily taken over by the army. Phantom soldiers have been seen and heard drilling. Occasionally the uniformed ghost of a Continental soldier walks past visitors, who may mistake it for one of the period costumed staff. Major General Anthony Wayne, whose lively ghost seems to be everywhere in Pennsylvania, sometimes appears on the grounds. Wayne worked with Washington during the encampment.

The enlisted men lived in log huts, which were destroyed when the farmer owners of the lands reclaimed them after the army departed. Replicas stand today.

Farm houses were taken over by the enlisted men, and they are now set up as mini-museums. Many of the farmers were Quakers, and it is easy to imagine how upset they were at having their homes turned into wartime quarters.

The house used by Washington as his headquarters teemed with so many people that they had to sleep on the floors and stairs. A few ghostly whispers survive in presences sensed by some, and the occasional unexplained noise can be heard.

The ghosts at Valley Forge are much more subtle than at Gettysburg, where violent fighting raged and the death toll was high. The historic park is well worth a visit, however. The best way to tune to the ghosts is to pay attention to subtle cues for invisible presences and the "feel" of the atmosphere. Dusk is often a good time to glimpse phantom soldiers out in the open fields.

WESTERN
PENNSYLVANIA

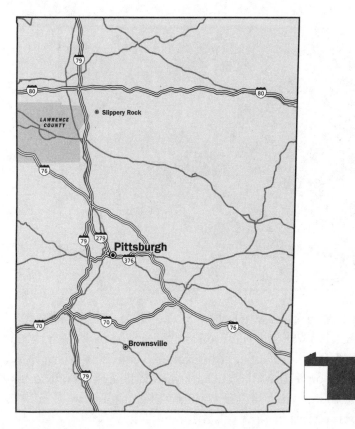

Brownsville
  Nemacolin Castle

Lawrence County
  McConnell's Mill State Park

Pittsburgh
  National Aviary
  Pittsburgh Playhouse

Slippery Rock
  Old Stone House

CHAPTER 24

McConnell's Mill State Park
LAWRENCE COUNTY

LOCATED IN LAWRENCE COUNTY, McConnell's Mill State Park is a National Natural Landmark. The park covers 2,546 acres and includes Slippery Rock Creek Gorge. The gristmill, for which McConnell's Mill State Park was named, is actually one of the first rolling mills in the country. The original mill, built in 1852, burned in a fire and was then rebuilt in 1868. For decades it processed corn, wheat, oats, and buckwheat for locals in the area under the ownership of the McConnell family. The state acquired the land and officially dedicated the park in October 1957.

The old mill isn't the only attraction of historical significance in the park. Just a stone's throw from the mill stands the old Howe Truss design covered bridge, built in 1874. The bridge crosses Slippery Rock Creek and is still used by those driving through the park today and has been named a National Historic Landmark. Many say that the area in the park around the old mill is home to several spirits that still make themselves known to visitors.

One of these spirits is that of a former mill worker and caretaker, Moses Wharton. Son of freed slaves from North Carolina, he came to work at the mill in 1880, when he was twenty. He delivered flour and feed to local stores in the area, and, after the mill closed in 1928, he served as caretaker. Moses would tend to the horses, and eventually cars, of the picnickers and sightseers who would visit the mill. The locals loved Moses, and he was well known for his sense of humor and playing a joke every now and then. He lived in his little cottage near the mill until he was ninety-two years old, and could not live on his own any longer. At that time he moved into the local County Home and remained there until he passed away at the ripe old age of ninety-four. Today it is believed that Moses is still watching over the old mill, and he supposedly chases people away from the place that he cared for so much in life.

Another ghostly legend tells of a girl who died in a car accident while crossing the covered bridge beside the mill. As the legend goes, her ghost can be summoned by parking your car on the bridge and then turning off your engine and headlights. When you honk your car horn three times she will appear in the car's rear view mirror. When one turns around to look she's never there.

Back when the mill was still operational, a particular man who worked there always took the same path to work. He would carry his lunch in a box and a lantern as well. As the story goes, the man died when there was a malfunction with some equipment in the mill. On some nights if you park your car near the mill, you can see him walking down the path on the hill towards the mill. When he enters the mill you can see a light from within and screams can be heard coming from inside the mill.

It's been said that a good many people have lost their lives in Slippery Rock Creek, which compared to most local creeks, is more like a small river. A good number of young, brave, if not foolhardy, individuals have drowned in the water. There were some who have met their demise while climbing on the park's large and enticing rock formations, too.

When one first sees McConnell's Mill from the outside, it is difficult to imagine the history that it contains on the inside. At least that was my impression when I first saw the mill. I was quite impressed by how well preserved things are inside. When you first enter, you feel the history contained within. With period-accurate tools, artifacts, and furniture, some of which actually belonged to the mill, you get a real sense of what it was like back when the mill was operational.

I was rather surprised to find that the mill has not just one, but two, basement levels. The upper basement level is where the farmers would bring in their bags of wheat, corn, and other crops to have it processed. There's a small room there where they would wait for it to be processed, a farmer's waiting room of sorts. The level below that is where the water, diverted in from Slippery Rock Creek, enters the mill to turn the turbines.

I can understand why someone who spent so much of their life tending to the mill would still be attached to it, even in the afterlife, whether that person is Moses Wharton, a McConnell, or perhaps someone else.

Ghosts are seen and felt during the daytime, and the figure with the lantern is seen at dusk, an auspicious time to notice phantoms. At night, I found the park takes on an eerie, mysterious, and spooky feel. The pathway walked by the lantern man is partially lined by sheer rock that evoke Jonathan Harker's ride to Castle Dracula.

During an investigation of the mill on a cool summer evening, paranormal investigators Denise Leithauser and Tom Harter had a possible paranormal experience while in the lower basement. It occurred late at night while they were doing some EVP work there with fellow investigator Bryan Barnes. They each experienced the same thing simultaneously. As they were standing in the center of the room, Tom spoke out that he suddenly felt the hairs on the back of his neck stand up while getting the sensation of goose bumps and a noticeable chill. Once that was said, Denise commented that she felt that exact same thing. Bryan, however, felt nothing, even though the three were all standing within three to four feet of each other.

The investigators were monitoring their equipment during this experience and saw that it lasted only about fifteen seconds. On an investigation, frequent measurements are made of temperature and electromagnetic field fluctuations, which are associated with paranormal phenomena. There was no change in either, despite the profound feeling of a chill.

Later in the evening, while they were on the upper basement level where the milling work would have once been done, Denise thought that she heard footsteps coming from the side of the mill nearest the creek, in the corner by the stairs that go down to the lower level. The three investigators were all together on the other side of the floor, near the stairs going up. Unfortunately, neither Tom nor Bryan heard them. Could this have been a sign that someone is still tending to the mill?

The amount of history known about the mill shows how important it is to the local history of the area. So, if there is a restless spirit or two still watching over it, I would think that they would be very pleased with how well it is being taken care of. No wonder one might chose not to leave.

It isn't hard to find something to do at McConnell's Mill State Park, with things like fishing and hiking, to whitewater rafting and kayaking, or even rappelling down the cliffs. And, for some out there, looking for ghosts.

Spotlight on Ghosts:
The Black Cross

Not far from the city of Butler in Butler County lies a heart-tugging, haunted monument to an untold number of people buried anonymously in the earth: The Black Cross. It lies near a quiet road in the rural woods, mute testimony to the cruelty of life and death only a century ago.

In the 19th century, most poor immigrants who came to Pennsylvania worked in the mines. The work was dangerous and took lives, but many believed that if you could survive the mines, you could survive just about anything. Tragically, that was not the case for one group of immigrants.

In the late 1800s, the immigrant mine workers were being transported by wagon to a new location. Influenza was sweeping through Butler County and many of them became severely ill. The wagon broke down. Before it could be repaired and the journey continued, many of the sick immigrants expired.

A large pit was dug, and their bodies were placed in it. They remained through the years, buried anonymously in a mass grave with little ceremony. A large black cross was erected at the spot.

In ghost lore, those who are not buried properly become restless in their graves. They do not go peacefully to the afterlife, but remain stuck, haunting the living. For years, the Black Cross has been known for its strange howling sounds, eerie mists, unusually chilling breezes and winds, and sad, whispering voices both heard audibly and captured on EVP. "Go that way," the voices murmur, and "pain" and "help us."

A historical marker stands at the spot today, along with a wooden cross and personal mementoes left by visitors moved to do something to honor these forlorn dead.

I visited there on a cold and steel-gray afternoon. The air at the site seemed thick and heavy, and I had a sense of the dead calling out from their grave.

The Black Cross is about 13.4 miles from Butler. From town, go north on North Main Street/PA8 for 1.2 miles, then take a slight right turn onto US-422 toward Kittanning. In 9.6 miles turn right at Cornetti Road/T830. Go 2.6 miles and turn right at Sasse Road/T618. You will see the marker from the road; it is a short walk into a clearing. Take a flower, leave a small gift, say a prayer. Help the dead!

CHAPTER 25

Pittsburgh Playhouse
PITTSBURGH

THEATERS HAVE REPUTATIONS for being haunted, and the Pittsburgh Playhouse is no exception. The theater has an unusual history that undoubtedly adds to its supernatural lore. It has evolved through a number of incarnations over the past century, and now is the performing arts center of Point Park University in the Oakland section of town. An estimated thirty thousand patrons attend performances here every year.

There are ghosts aplenty in the theater, including actors and actresses who performed there, white lady apparitions, a weeping ghost, and even an entity called the "Bouncing Red Meanie." No backstage tours are offered, so the best way to take in the phenomena is to attend a play and pay attention to what goes on around you beyond the stage.

What is it about theaters that make so many of them haunted? I have my own theory, after years of investigating and researching them. Many hauntings are tied to intense, emotional events. A theater is a focal point of emotions. The actors, actresses, and production staff are intertwined in the emotional intensity of the production, whether it be a drama, musical, or comedy. The actors must summon emotions from deep within and convey them to the audiences, who in turn are emotionally engaged in whatever takes place on stage. Day after day of rehearsals, night after night of performances cause the emotions to build, layer upon layer. Thus, it is no surprise that ghostly residues become part of "atmosphere," and perhaps even the structure of a theater itself. Come to a theater, and you are in a time machine of emotions past and present.

I arrived at the Pittsburgh Playhouse on a warm June afternoon after the close of the season, and was graciously met by Alfred Kirschman, the properties manager, and Beverly Weber, the director of finance. Kirschman, who has been associated with the playhouse for many years, gave me a thorough tour and relayed some of the Playhouse's colorful history.

The Playhouse actually houses four theaters, each belonging to a different era. The oldest part of the theater is the Rauh, much smaller, which once was a German beer hall and social club around the turn of the twentieth century. It was originally called the Haml Street Theater. In the 1930s, the building was acquired and renamed by the Richard S. Rauh family of entrepreneurs and actors. Richard's wife, Helen Wayne Rauh, was a popular Pittsburgh actress. Their son, Richard E. Rauh, became an actor, teacher, and philanthropist, and in 2005 was awarded the Pittsburgh New Works Festival Lifetime Achievement Award.

The main auditorium is now the Rockwell Theater, once the Tree of Life Synagogue. The synagogue stood next door to the Rauh, and was added to the playhouse when the temple moved to new quarters and vacated its building. The auditorium has a spectacular domed ceiling from its synagogue days. The altar was once where the stage is now.

There are two small studio theaters downstairs used for try-out productions.

Dressing rooms were built where row houses once stood—allegedly a brothel was among them. The dressing rooms are small and plain and have served many famous actors, such as Lillian Russell of yesteryear and Jane Alexander of modern times.

The theater once had a fashionable restaurant in its lower level; the space is used for storage today.

No wonder the Pittsburgh Playhouse has so many ghosts! Synagogue, beer hall, theaters, row houses, and perhaps even a brothel have all poured their emotional history into the place. Ghostly things happen throughout the theater, but are concentrated in the Rockwell and Rauh theaters, and in the dressing room area.

The cast of phantom characters includes:

– John Johns, an actor who performed at the Playhouse throughout the 1950s and who died in his dressing room, originally Number 6 (now Number 7) in 1960. There are different versions of his demise. According to one, he collapsed, possibly of a heart attack, after a performance and died before an ambulance arrived. Another version says he collapsed after attending a banquet in the restaurant downstairs, where he possibly had a bad meal.

    The ghost of Johns is heard climbing the steps to his old dressing room where it stops at the threshold. He also walks up and down the dressing room hallway. Actors and students glimpse him, dressed in an old-fashioned tuxedo, checking sets and props.

Seats in the main auditorium have name plaques on them. Some are for actors and some are the names of generous donors and patrons. The seat bearing the name of John Johns reportedly depresses on its own during a performance if the ghost of Johns is present. The seat is not always in the main auditorium, as it is in one of the front rows that are sometimes removed for extended set designs.

– A Lady in White is believed to be an unnamed actress who performed in the old Hamlet Street Theater during the 1930s. Her story is probably more legend than fact. According to lore, she was married in the old synagogue. During the reception, she discovered to her horror that her new husband was having an affair. She dashed up the steps to the balcony and threw herself off to her death. Another version of the story says that she raced up to the balcony and then shot herself, although where and how she grabbed a gun is not explained. Nonetheless, some see her ghost walking across the balcony with the gun still in her hand. She is also seen standing on the theater stage from time to time. She has allegedly been captured in at least one photograph taken in one of the light projection booths.

– Weeping Eleanor is a ghost who is heard but never seen. The story goes that a fire in the row houses (now the site of dressing rooms) claimed her life and that of her daughter. Her invisible ghost weeps uncontrollably in the dressing room area.

– Gorgeous George is anything but handsome. This ghost is ugly, with a contorted green and rotting face. His story is not known, nor is the reason why he haunts the theater. Gorgeous George sneaks up behind people, taps on windows, and pokes people's shoulders to frighten them.

– The Bouncing Red Meanie is one of the more intriguing phantoms at the Playhouse. He appears mostly in the Rockwell Theater as a red-colored man who paces around as though agitated. He also appears as a ball of red light that bounces off walls and flies through the air. The Bouncing Red Meanie was first reported on Halloween night in 1974 during a séance at the Playhouse held by a group of students. The red figure appeared about ten minutes into the séance. Did the students conjure a ghost already in the theater but not known, or did they invite in a brand new resident? No one knows for certain, but the Bouncing Red Meanie has taken up residence at the Playhouse. He is known to play mean tricks on people by startling them or giving them a push, and has been said to have pushed a ladder out from underneath a staff person.

– An unknown presence on the steps leading to the ladies' room in the main theater area makes some people feel uncomfortable.

In addition, the balcony of the Rockwell has a "heavy" feeling to some people.

Kirschman has had a variety of experiences over the years. "I've always felt a presence in this building, but I've never felt threatened by it," he said. "If there are ghosts, I've always tried to communicate with them."

Kirschman once worked as the house manager, opening and closing the building. In the morning, he arrived before anyone else and was alone in the building for a while.

One area he unlocked held the administrative offices. At the time, the phones were big, push-button models, with rows of lighted buttons on the bottom for multiple call lines. "One morning I came in and went into one of the offices, and saw that the phone had all five or six buttons lit," said Kirschman. "I knew that in order for them to all be lit, someone had to be on all those lines. And I knew I was the only one in the building. So I picked up the phone and heard multi-level conversations, one over the top of the other. I tried every button and got the same thing."

Kirschman said into the phone, "Hello? Hello?" But no one talking paid him any attention, nor could he understand anything being said. The voices were breathy, and whatever they were saying was all a jumble. "Hello? Hello?" Still, no response.

"It didn't go away for a good ten minutes," he said. "Then the lights just went off all at once. It was kind of scary." It never happened again, at least to his knowledge. Were spirits of the dead having a party line phone fest? Phone calls from the dead are a known paranormal phenomenon.

On another occasion, Kirschman was locking up for the night. He locked the two main accesses to the building and was in the process of locking up the administrative office area when a male voice boomed out of thin air behind him, "Alfred! Hey, Alfred!" Kirschman turned, but no one was present. Who was the mysterious man hailing him? "I took it to be Gorgeous George, who likes to sneak up behind people," Kirschman said.

"There have been other things, too," he went on. "Doors in the dressing rooms have jiggled on me. When I was locking up in that area, I would walk down the hall saying out loud, 'I'm locking up, okay, get out of the rooms now.' The door handles of the dressing rooms would jiggle by themselves.

"I used to paint scenery at night by myself. I would hear moaning sounds all night. It may have been air in the pipes, but it did sound like a person moaning. I would say, 'What's the matter, what are you trying to tell me?' I never got any answer."

Kirschman introduced me to Dennis Deasis, who works on the housekeeping and maintenance staff. Deasis has been spooked a number of times while working by himself in the theater late at night or early in the morning. Normally, he prefers to work alone, but the ghostly phenomena at the theater have caused him to alter his hours.

"I was doing a project late one night, stripping the floor down in the basement," Deasis told me. "I told the guard to lock everything up. Before he left, I walked around with him to make sure everything was locked up. I went downstairs and started the stripping and waxing. Around midnight or one o'clock in the morning, I went back upstairs to get my lunch. I found the door to the upstairs wide open. I know for a fact that the guard locked the door, and there was nobody here except for me. I was shocked. I thought maybe the guard forgot something and came back, but the light was off upstairs."

Deasis called out, "Is anybody here?" There was no answer. Chilled in a peculiar way, he went around, and screamed out repeatedly, "Is anybody here?"

Silence.

Deasis looked at me, shook his head and laughed. "It was a moment where all my hair stood up," he said. "There was no way that door could be open. I decided to leave, and I went home. Ever since then, I don't stay past midnight."

He also now prefers to arrive in the morning when a guard will be present. "There were a couple of times when I came in at four or five o'clock in the morning, and I'd be here by myself," he said. "I would hear footsteps and knocking on the walls. Sometimes when I'd be waxing or buffing the floor, a wind, like a person walking, would go past and I got chilled. I'd be cleaning dressing rooms and would hear footsteps. I didn't know that an actor had died in one of the rooms until Alfred told me. That was spooky.

"I kind of got used to it," Deasis said. "Sometimes I would bring a radio to void the noise. Now, I don't work here by myself anymore. I make sure that at least the guard is here."

Spotlight on Ghosts:
Phone Calls from the Dead

When ghosts want to reach out and touch someone, it's not always with a tap on the shoulder. Sometimes they use high technology. They pick up the phone and call.

"Phone calls from the dead" is a mysterious phenomenon that has been documented since the telephone was invented in the late nineteenth century by Alexander Graham Bell. These calls usually occur randomly and without warning, sometimes right after a person has died and sometimes months later, especially on an anniversary date like a death, birthday, or marriage, or on a holiday.

The recipient picks up the phone and often hears a great deal of static, as though the call is coming from a long, long distance, or there is weather interfering on the line. The voice at the other end may identify himself or herself, or may simply start talking. Even though the identity of the caller may be recognized, the voice will sound strange, perhaps a bit tinny, or carrying an unusual cadence to the words. "Hello, Mom is that you?" A phantom caller may repeat over and over again.

Sometimes recipients are so shocked they do not know what to say, and the call ends abruptly. Sometimes they speak, but the caller does not respond to their words, and keeps repeating a phrase, eventually fading away. And in some cases, recipients do not know the caller is dead, and they try to carry on a normal conversation. In rare cases, such a call can last up to half an hour. The recipients are shocked to learn later that their caller was ringing them from beyond!

No good explanation exists for how and why phone calls from the dead can take place. Most of them involve people who have had strong emotional ties. Perhaps the telephone somehow provides the most efficient way to get one last message across the Great Divide.

CHAPTER 26

National Aviary
PITTSBURGH

THE NATIONAL AVIARY in Pittsburgh is testimony to the fact that anything can become haunted—even a zoo for birds. There are no phantom birds flying around the building, but plenty of other odd things go on, both day and night.

The National Aviary is little-known as a haunted location. In July 2009, I was part of an investigation group that was only the second such group ever given access to the facility. The night was organized by the International Parapsychology Research Foundation, Inc., founded by Brian and Jennifer Schill. We were first given a tour by a staff guide, Erin, who had worked at the aviary for eight years. "There are an awful lot of strange things that happen here from time to time," she said.

Perhaps it is no surprise that the aviary is haunted, considering its history. From 1826 to 1880, part of the site was occupied by the Western State Penitentiary, the western counterpart to Eastern State Penitentiary in Philadelphia. It was a kinder, gentler, and smaller prison than its famous sister. During the Civil War, WSP housed Confederate officers captured in the South. There were no deaths recorded at the prison.

The prison was torn down to make way for Pittsburgh's first plant conservatory. The conservatory was destroyed by a natural gas explosion in the late 1920s. In 1952 it was rebuilt by the City of Pittsburgh, and birds were added to the indoor gardens. It eventually became solely an aviary, with additions made through the 1990s until the facility had more than twenty-five thousand square feet of exhibit space. The Aviary was one of the first zoos to feature free-flight rooms in which visitors could share space with birds.

In the 1980s, the Aviary began concentrating on wildlife conservation through captive breeding of rare and endangered birds. Lack of funds threatened its closure by 1991. A group of citizens formed Save the Aviary, Inc., a private, nonprofit corporation, and privatized the aviary in 1992. It was given honorary national status and was renamed the National Aviary.

The aviary has several haunted hot spots. One is the Wetlands Room, which houses birds from North and South Americas. "A man who had been working here for about ten years was in here cleaning, hosing down the room, when all of a sudden he heard a loud banging noise coming from the basement below," said Erin. "It was so loud that it shook the floor. He went downstairs to see what was causing it. He couldn't find anything wrong. He never figured it out."

Loud banging noises emanating from the basements—there are more than one basement rooms—happen periodically. During the first paranormal investigation, banging sounds came from beneath the Tropical Rain Forest Room. "There were four to five bangs, and they were so loud you could almost feel them," said Erin. "I have never heard anything like that, and I don't know what could have caused it."

People downstairs in the basements have heard footsteps walking on the floors above at times when no one is upstairs in any of the bird rooms. At times throughout the facility, staff members feel as though they are being watched. The presences are benign.

Some people have seen a mysterious red light. "I was here late one night with a coworker," explained Erin. "We were bringing back some birds that we had out on a community outreach event. When we walked by the eagle exhibit to go into the courtyard, we noticed there was a strange red light floating around. We walked back behind the exhibit, and we even got up on the roof to see where it was coming from. We weren't sure if it was a warning light from the exhibit. It floated above the eagles and we never could figure out what it was."

The strangest event that happened to Erin took place in the kitchen. "I was here early one morning about three in the morning chopping vegetables and getting the diets ready before anyone else came in. I was by myself and had my back to the wall. The radio behind me turned on and off by itself. When I turned around to look, I saw that it was unplugged." That was unnerving, she added.

It is not uncommon for cameras and battery-operated equipment to malfunction in haunted places, and they do at the aviary. "A few years ago we had a Halloween event called wine and spirits," Erin said. "We hired a storyteller to come in and tell ghost stories, and we gave tours. Staff members went along on the tours. At one point, two staff members were shining their flashlights to show the way, and their lights went dead at the same time. They had to put new batteries in."

Erin said she had never seen any Civil War prisoner ghosts at the Aviary, though she has heard reports that some visitors have glimpsed apparitions in war-era clothing.

As part of our investigation, I had brought my Frank's Box, a device that rapidly scans the radio and creates a jumble of sound that is intended to facilitate real-time EVP. The box operator asks questions, and sometimes direct answers pop out that are not coming from snippets of radio broadcast. Frank's Box research is controversial, but an exciting and growing part of paranormal research and investigation. I have been using them for several years, and have gotten communications that I cannot explain naturally.

I especially wanted to set up the box in the kitchen where Erin had had her most unusual experience. She was glad to accompany us. We got it running and I started asking for any communicators to make themselves known. A male voice said there were six communicators present. The communicators said they knew Erin and other staff members, some of whom they named correctly. One communicator said he had been the one to turn the radio on and off and had done so in order to get attention. The communicators said they liked the staff members and the birds, too, and sometimes followed the staff around on their duties.

The communicators did not identify themselves, so it is not known if they had past connections to the aviary or to the site, or were "visitors" drawn to the aviary for other reasons. But the short conversation we had with them made for an exciting evening.

If you visit the aviary intending on experiencing ghosts as well as birds, go early or late when visitor activity is likely to be light. The exotic birds can be noisy, but they quiet down towards dusk. Pay attention when you walk down the hallways, for presences have been sensed there as well as in the atriums. If you have an experience, let a staff person know so that you can contribute to the haunted history of this beautiful establishment.

CHAPTER 27

Old Stone House
SLIPPERY ROCK

THERE ARE NOT MANY PLACES from Colonial times left in southwestern Pennsylvania, and there are even fewer that come with their own resident ghost. However, the Old Stone House in Slippery Rock, Butler County, fits both those criteria. You will find it just off William Flynn Highway and not too far from Moraine State Park.

Originally built by John K. Brown in 1822 out of local sandstone, the Stone House, as it was called then, served as a tavern and wayside inn. The isolated place became a common stop for travelers en route from Pittsburgh to Erie, as well as a haven for local lumbermen and highwaymen, too. The countryside was rough and wild in those days, full of black bears, bandits,

Indians, and more. The Pittsburgh-to-Erie trip took thirty-six hours, and a lot of dreadful things could happen along the way. The Stone House provided a bit of relief and comfort.

The inn operated until 1885, and famous people passed through its doors. According to tradition, the Marquis de Lafayette visited the Stone House shortly after it opened. Lafayette was an ally to Washington during the Revolutionary War.

During the Civil War, a Pennsylvania regiment formed at the Stone House. After the war, the development of railroads decreased the wagon trade, and the Stone House began to lose patrons. In 1885, it was rented out as a private house, then later was abandoned. It fell into ruins.

Thankfully, the structure was saved by the Pennsylvania Historical and Museum Commission in 1963 and reconstructed in the early 1960s. An attempt was made to use as much original material as possible, but liberties were taken with some needed updates. An addition was added onto one side of the inn, which contains the office, electricity was run throughout, and stairs to the second floor were added on the inside, as well as a basement.

The former inn was turned over to Slippery Rock University in the early 1980s, and since then has been used by the university as a museum for educational and community purposes. It is now a Historical Landmark, and the university continues to offer tours to the public, and host craft fairs, period military reenactments and encampments there.

The house is plainly furnished for visitors today. When I visited it, I had a hard time imagining that it had been the scene of unspeakable violence. One of the worst crimes that ever happened in Butler County is linked back to the Old Stone House, and is believed to account for some of its paranormal activity. It happened at the end of June 1843 and involved a well-known local Native American, Sam Mohawk, who lived on the Seneca

Reservation in Cattarauga, New York. Mohawk made frequent trips down the Allegheny Valley, where he was known as "the terror of the region" for his alcoholic binges and raging behavior.

Mohawk had descended upon Butler County going from inn to inn demanding whiskey, but he was refused everywhere. He went into a rage and so terrified the locals that they collected money to put him on a stagecoach to Meadville. He disappeared off the stage around the Stone House. At midnight he appeared and demanded whiskey and the sum of money that had been raised for his wagon fare. The manager, John Sills, drove him off with a club.

Sometime during the night, Mohawk made his way up the road from the Stone House to the home of farmer James Wigton and family. There he took out his rage upon the helpless family and bludgeoned to death Mrs. Wigton and their five children. James Wigton was not home at that time. The farmer had gotten up at daybreak to travel to the nearby home of his father. Meanwhile, Wigton's brother, John, who lived a mile away, saw Mohawk pass by around dawn. He then went to James's house to borrow a wagon. He made the grisly discovery of the bodies, which had been piled in a bloody heap in the kitchen. All of them had their brains beaten out with a large stone, which was left on the floor. Mrs. Wigton, thirty, was partially dressed. The five children, ages eight, five, four, three, and one, were in their night clothes.

James Wigton was gone only a few hours, but when he returned at eight o'clock in the morning, he found a crowd of people gathered around his house. Rushing up, he was prevented from entering and was given the shocking news. Wigton was so stunned that he fell unconscious for three days.

Sam Mohawk continued his violent rage, attacking others with stones and beating them senseless. He was finally stopped when a man knocked him unconscious with a flail. Mohawk confessed to the murders, describing how Mrs. Wigton had begged him to spare her children. He made her watch him kill three of them before killing her. Mohawk was tried and executed by hanging. James Wigton witnessed the hanging.

The majority of the paranormal activity that has been reported at the Old Stone House has come from the graduate students and volunteers from Slippery Rock University that volunteer there. Once account that I heard from several sources tells of a volunteer who locked up one night, only to return the next morning to find that some dominoes that are kept out on one of the tables in the tavern room were arranged to spell out the words—straight out of a Hollywood horror film—"GET OUT." Of course, this wasn't how the dominoes were left the night before, and there had been no one else inside prior to the volunteer returning that next morning.

There have been many reports by people who have heard the sound of someone walking on the stairs to the second floor. Thinking that perhaps someone came in for a tour and just wandered up there, they go to check it out. However, to their surprise, they find no one up there or anywhere else. People outside the building have reported seeing an apparition of a woman through the window in the west bedroom. She supposedly wears an old dress dating to possibly the eighteenth or nineteenth century. No one has given a clear description of her face. Speculation is that the ghost is the murdered Mrs. Wigton. From the inside, there have been reports of shuffling noises that come from that very same room. Years ago, some students from the university were spending the night in the Old Stone House and allegedly captured a "groaning noise" on a tape recorder while in the west bedroom.

A dark shadowy figure—Sam Mohawk?—has been reported on the grounds near the house.

Investigators from The Center for Paranormal Study and Investigation (CPSI) have conducted at least four separate paranormal investigations at the Old Stone House. During the first investigation the group founder, Tom Harter, had set out to see if any of these stories about the events in the west bedroom could be documented. Along with the deployment of the usual infrared cameras and audio recorders, he set up a passive infrared motion detector in there. At one point in the night, when the room was closed off with no one in there, the motion detector went off.

They captured some EVP on their second investigation. With a digital voice recorder that was set up in the middle room on the second floor, they caught two different recordings. According to Bryan Barnes, CPSI case manger, the best was a repeating of words that Tom had originally spoken. Just a few seconds after Tom said, "...they were walking, up the path..." a deep, whispery voice repeated, "walking...the path."

It has become a tradition over the years for the university to put on a free Halloween ghost story event each year just before Halloween. They welcome, and encourage, the public to come to this free event to listen to ghost stories told by volunteers from the university's theater department and revolutionary war recreationists, and to hear about true paranormal events and investigations from members of CPSI.

When you visit the Old Stone House, take some time to linger in the rooms and try to tune in to the "atmosphere." Walk around the property and do the same. Horrific events often seem to impress themselves into the very space and air of haunted places, and by paying attention you may hear or feel ghostly phenomena from the past.

Spotlight on Ghosts: Ghost Ships and Lake Spirits of Erie

Phantom ships ply the waters of the world everywhere: oceans, seas, lakes and rivers. Many a sailor has seen them, grim testimonies to tragedies at the hands of water and weather, and sometimes war.

The most haunted waterways of America are the Great Lakes, where fast-rising, powerful storms can sink even a huge ship in minutes. Lake Erie, considered one of the most treacherous of the Great Lakes, has a number of ghostly ships sailing on journeys that never end.

Several ghost ships were the victims of a steel ship named the *Northern Queen*, commissioned in 1889. The *Northern Queen* somehow accidentally rammed and sank three ships on lakes Erie and Huron: the *Fayette Brown*, the *North Star*, and the *Grammar*. Bad judgment, fog and unknown factors were at play. In the 1920s, the *Northern Queen* fell victim herself, sinking in a storm. The ship was raised and cut into scrap.

Another ghost ship is the *Radiant*, a schooner that set out across Lake Erie and vanished without explanation or trace.

On December 1909, the *Marquette and Bessamer No. 2*, a car ferry loaded with 30 rail cars of coal and steel, went down in a storm, taking all hands with her. The ship was bound for Port Stanley, a Canadian port, and nearly made it. A sudden storm and high winds prevented it from making safe harbor, and those on the shore could hear the shrill sounds of its distress whistle. The ship turned back to Ohio, but never made it there, either. Three days after the ship went down, search parties discovered a lone lifeboat with nine frozen corpses in it.

Since then, the ghostly, old-fashioned whistle of the ship is heard by sailors on other ships, and its phantom form has been seen slowly crawling back and forth across the lake as its phantom crew searches in vain for safety.

Two islands in Lake Erie are haunted. Kelly Island, mined for limestone, was the site of a mine explosion in the 1840s that killed many miners. Sailors traveling around the island claimed that ghosts of the dead men tore holes in the bottoms of their ships.

Johnson Island was used as a prison camp for Confederate soldiers during the Civil War. At its peak, it held about 15,000 prisoners. Many died in the inhospitable climate. Their ghosts create a sense of unease on the island, and some visitors say they hear the sounds of "Dixie" being played.

CHAPTER 28

Nemacolin Castle
BROWNSVILLE

NEMACOLIN CASTLE SITS ATOP A HILL in Brownsville, Fayette County, commanding an impressive view of the
Monongahela River. A long history stretching back to pre-Colo-
nial Indian cultures may contribute to its haunting activity.

The Monongahela Valley is part of the Upper Ohio Valley,
an area settled by the mound-building Adena People two thousand to three thousand years ago. Nemacolin was built on one
of the old mound sites, which were used for Adena burials. It
was named after Nemacolin, a Native American who occupied
the area and aided the early white settlers making their way
along what is now Route 40. Brownsville was an important

trading and industry site in the migration of settlers into the Ohio Valley.

The original part of the castle was built in 1789 by Jacob Bowman, a pioneer merchant from Hagerstown, Maryland. Bowman established a frontier trading post on the approximate site of Old Fort Burd near Brownsville. An astute business-man, he built two prosperous wrought iron nail factories. He acquired numerous pieces of property and was an important figure in Brownsville. In 1795 President George Washington named Bowman Brownsville's first postmaster.

Bowman's original house was small and crude; Jacob believed in putting his money into building his business empire. Three generations of Bowmans lived at Nemacolin, and later descendants added to Jacob's house. In the 1850s, Nelson Bowman made the structure what it is today. Nemacolin is one of about two dozen large structures from this period still stand-ing in western Pennsylvania. Its twenty-two rooms reflect early Colonial to late Victorian living and the later Bowmans' free-wheeling spending. Many of the furnishings are original to the family. Since the 1960s the castle has been owned and main-tained by the Brownsville Historical Society, and it is on the National Register of Historic Places.

Entering Nemacolin is like stepping back in time. History, however, may not be the only thing that one experiences there. The castle has earned quite a reputation of being haunted. The Bowman family was the only family to ever live in this house. The "imprints" of their past are quite strong, and it is easy to see why so many people have had paranormal experiences there, even on tours. Add to it the history of Indian burials and you have a good mix for hauntings. No Indian ghosts are seen at Nemacolin, but burial sites are often associated with paranor-mal phenomena.

At least ten ghosts have been reported at Nemacolin. The two most prominent are Elizabeth, who seems like a very proper lady wearing a white dress, and Mary, a seven-year-old girl with dark, curly hair. Elizabeth, dressed in white, has been witnessed screaming and running in the house. She disappears into rooms.

It is believed by many that some of the other ghosts who haunt the once luxurious home are the Bowman family members themselves, or perhaps some of the staff who had spent so much of their life working for, and tending to, the family. One ghost is a woman wearing a dark dress with her hair pulled back who is seen frequently in the second floor hallway. Some people have seen a man, thought to be Jacob Bowman himself, in the library and a male spirit has been reported in the basement, too. There may be spirits of children still lingering within the walls of Nemacolin Castle. One, or more, of whom may be the four children of Nelson Bowman that died there.

A ghost of a little girl has been seen in the nursery that is just off of the master bedroom. In this same room toys have been known to move on their own, and a little girl's laughter has been heard. Things even tend to move from one place to another in there. I learned that volunteers there have seen objects sitting on a shelf, and then only minutes later, would find them lying on the floor. Sometimes, they are found all the way over on the other side of the nursery without any explanation.

Many people have reported hearing voices within the home, even when no one else was around. It's not uncommon for people to hear doors slamming shut or the sound of footsteps throughout the place. There are unexplained cold spots and smells.

One staff person related that a phantom dog has been heard barking.

Paranormal investigator Bryan Barnes had an interesting experience while investigating with his group here. As they were wrapping up their investigation for the night, he heard what sounded like footsteps running up, or possibly down, the main staircase in the house. He went up the steps to investigate and found another team member who had already been up there sitting and taking pictures. She heard the footsteps, too, but once she saw Bryan, she thought that it was he she had just heard. Once he explained to her what he had heard, they both realized that they had both heard the same thing.

"I thought it was Tom and Pete going up the stairs," Barnes said, referring to two other members of the team. "I was surprised when I found out that they weren't even up there."

Others on his team had some experiences of their own that night, too, including investigators Heidi Szedon and Paula Lieberum, who had several unexplained readings on their EMF meters.

During another investigation, paranormal investigator Tom Harter and his team had some possible communication with an unknown spirit in the castle's library. While conducting an EVP session, they requested any type of interaction from spirits willing to communicate. Harter asked that they make a noise, such as knocking on something. Immediately, Tom and his team heard two knocks.

NORTHERN
PENNSYLVANIA

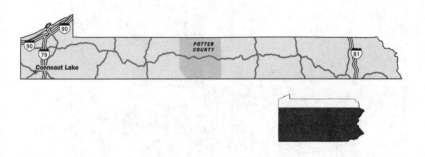

Conneaut Lake
   Hotel Conneaut
Potter County
   Ole Bull State Park and Black Forest

CHAPTER 29

Hotel Conneaut
CONNEAUT LAKE

IN THE NINETEENTH CENTURY, Conneaut Lake was a highly desired recreation and vacation site in Crawford County, northwestern Pennsylvania, close to the Ohio border. For more than a century, the area has attracted pleasure seekers. Some of them found tragedy instead of pleasure and seem to have become ghosts.

The town of Conneaut Lake was originally founded in 1799 as Evansburg. In 1892 the town renamed itself after the neighboring lake. The same year, Exposition Park opened as a two-hundred-acre amusement center, and featured a grand resort Exposition Hotel. It was rebuilt as the Hotel Conneaut in 1902, and the park was renamed Conneaut Lake Park in 1919.

Celebrities stayed at the hotel, among them Mark Twain. At the height of its glory, the hotel had three hundred guest rooms, a huge dining room, a crystal ballroom, and luxury services. Rooms cost one dollar a night—a pricey sum for the day. At least a dozen resort hotels dotted the area. In 1925, the hotel was expanded to add another 150 rooms.

By the 1940s, the Hotel Conneaut was already into its faded glory days. In 1943, lightning struck the hotel and sparked a fire that destroyed a significant portion of the east wing, including about 150 guest rooms, the main dining room, and the main lobby. It was never rebuilt, and the hotel was remodeled back to 150 rooms. The park and hotel remained in operation until 2007, when they were closed due to lack of funds. They reopened in 2009, and ghost enthusiasts welcomed the news, for the hotel is renowned for its haunting activity.

The fire spawned the most famous ghost legend of the hotel, that of young Elizabeth, who was supposedly staying at the hotel that night. According to legend, she was to be married there the next day. She died in the fire while trying on her wedding dress. Another version of the story says Elizabeth was already married, and she and her husband were on their honeymoon at the hotel when the fire broke out, killing Elizabeth. Her fiancé or husband escaped, and she died while searching for him in the smoke-filled corridors. Different room numbers are assigned to the tragic young woman: 128 is most often cited, followed by 308, 321, and 324. Most likely, Elizabeth was not a real person—there is no record of a woman by that name dying in the 1943 fire.

Yet, the ghost of a young woman dressed in white is seen frequently in the old portions of the hotel on the second and third floors. She steps straight out of walls, bringing cold drafts, chills, and mists with her. Sometimes guests smell her jasmine or rose perfume and hear her mournful crying in the middle of the night. According to lore, if Elizabeth takes a dislike to a guest, she assaults him with an unpleasant smell.

Elizabeth is blamed for poltergeist activity, such as the movement and displacement of small objects, and camera malfunctions. She is not fond of weddings, perhaps because she did not have one of her own. Once the staff prepared for a wedding, only to find that the bed linens and towels had been torn off the beds and rods in all the rooms on the third floor, and piled into heaps on the floor.

Another story tells that a woman tried to make a call on a pay phone at the hotel, but the call would not go through. When she tried to get her coins back, a gold wedding band fell out instead. The guest certainly came out ahead on that one!

Elizabeth is fond of small children; another story about her says that she saved the life of a child in the fire. She is known to tuck in children who stay at the hotel, making certain their blankets are pulled up around them. Elizabeth is also seen in the dining room and ballroom; sometimes she is approached by people who mistake her for a real person until she vanishes.

Other ghosts living at the hotel or on the grounds are:

- An unnamed "crazy chef" who supposedly died in the same fire. He throws pots and pans around in the kitchen, and sometimes knives and candlesticks.

- John, who haunts the television lounge downstairs and turns on the television set.

- Ethel and Francis, a ghostly couple who dance continually in the ballroom. They are an old-fashioned couple; Francis is dressed in a tuxedo and Ethel in a pink ball gown with pearls. They love to dance to piano music. Some guests and staff have seen a couple in period clothing sitting on the lawn, or running down a corridor, as though trying to escape a fire.

- A Civil War soldier who lives in a tree by the hotel. He sits in the tree holding a lantern.

- A little blonde girl in a white dress who rides a tricycle. Lore holds that she died when her tricycle fell down stairs or off a balcony. The little girl zooms down hallways at guests. Her name is believed to be Angelina.
- Michael, a little boy who wanders about the hallways looking for his mother. His tear-stained face is pale, and he has dark circles under his eyes. When people try to help him, he disappears.
- Tommy, a vagrant who is dressed in a secondhand pinstriped suit dated to the 1930s or 40s. He is believed to have died of pneumonia after squatting in the cottages in the park. He was dressed in a secondhand suit and given a pauper's funeral. His ghost appears in the ballroom, and he often looks as though he is trying to get warm.
- Anonymous ghosts who rattle doorknobs, knock on doors, slam doors, turn lights on and off, climb into bed with people, shake beds, stand by bedsides, moan, and turn on faucets and showers.
- Voices who tell people to get out.
- Phantom animals, including kittens, a black and white cat, and a collie dog.

The grounds of the park have numerous ghosts as well, including Native Americans, ghostly horses and buggies, dancers, and mysterious lights.

Carrie Andra Pavlik is a former employee at the hotel who became so fascinated by the ghost stories that she collected them for years. The resort has an old-fashioned charm that draws people there. "It is as if everyone who ever walked through those doors over the past century has left a piece of themselves," she said. "It's an energy that can't be denied, even by a first-time visitor."

CHAPTER 30

Ole Bull State Park
POTTER COUNTY

THE WILDS OF NORTHERN PENNSYLVANIA held a special allure for a solo violinist of the nineteenth century. When Ole (pronounced Oh-lay) Borneman Bull visited the dense forests and spectacular hills of Potter County, he didn't see Pennsylvania—he saw a vision of his beloved native Norway. Bull was determined to recreate his homeland here, not just for himself, but for fellow Norwegians who emigrated to America. His vision was doomed, however. Bull's legacy was not a colony, but ruins haunted by ghosts.

Bull's name doesn't ring much of a bell today, but in the mid-nineteenth century, he was famous in Norway, and he toured internationally, including several trips to America. He became Norway's first international celebrity. Born in Bergen, Norway, in 1810, he was a child prodigy and could skillfully play folk tunes on the violin. A passionate nationalist throughout his life, he sought to promote Norway in every way possible. He especially featured Norwegian folk music in his concerts.

Bull made a fortune as a violinist, enough to buy 11,144 acres of land in Pennsylvania for $10,388 in 1853. The land was rugged and wild. The forests were thick, reminding him of European woods. The mountains folded in spectacular scenery, their sides plunging to Kettle Creek Valley reminiscent of Norway's fjords. Even the name of the area reminded him of Europe: the Black Forest.

Bull established four colonies, New Bergen, Oleana, New Norway, and Valhalla. At the highest point in Valhalla, he set about building a castle, Nordjenskald, as the centerpiece of his communities. He immediately attracted enthusiastic Norwegians who wanted to participate in his dream of the perfect places to live, little utopias where everyone would be happy.

But clearing the dense white pines and hemlocks proved to be more of a challenge than the immigrants anticipated. The first winter was severe. The remote location was difficult for supply wagons to reach. The conditions were so daunting that the castle was abandoned in less than a year, incomplete. The immigrants scattered, many of them migrating to Minnesota and the Dakotas. Bull returned to touring and giving concerts. In the late nineteenth century, the lumber industry purchased Bull's land, heavily logged the old-growth timber, and then abandoned the area. The Commonwealth of Pennsylvania purchased much of the land.

Today all that is left of Ole Bull's vision is the small, 132-acre Ole Bull State Park, located along Kettle Creek, surrounded by the Susquehannock State Forest. The park was established in 1925. The only remains of the castle are a pit where the foundation once was built. In 2002, the citizens of Norway paid for a statue of Bull to be erected in the park to mark the 150th anniversary of New Norway.

It seems that Bull never completely left his beloved Pennsylvania site. Many visitors to the ruins report the sounds of phantom fiddling and the voices of what may have been the men and women who sought to become Bull's pioneers.

The day I visited the ruins in the park, I had the place to myself. The scenery was breathtaking, and I could see how Bull fell in love with the land. I took out my digital recorder and asked questions, hoping to record some EVP. No phantom fiddling appeared, but when I asked "Did you like it here?" a faint, tinny male voice said in a clipped manner, "Hard work." Undoubtedly it was hard work to try to get the communities rooted and the castle built. Was it Bull himself who answered, or one of his would-be residents? There is no way to know. It seems that presences linger at the site, and ghostly voices are carried on the breezes. At one point, while walking about, I thought I heard footsteps crunching the ground behind me—but no one was there. Only the ghosts of the past remain.

While you're in the area, take Route 144 to just south of the castle at the Village of Cross Fork. Take the Twin Sisters hiking trail north for three miles to Twin Sisters' Hollow. At dusk, you may meet an apparition known as the Headless Frenchman. According to lore, he was a silver prospector who was killed by Indians in the 1600s. They chopped off his head, which his ghost carries beneath one arm. The ghost also appears at midnight of the full moon.

Spotlight on Ghosts:
Thunderbirds

Giant birds with wing spans up to sixty feet? Sounds like something out of the dinosaur age. But legendary giant, feathered birds called thunderbirds have been seen and recorded for hundreds of years into modern times, and certain areas of Pennsylvania are famous for being haunted by them.

Thunderbirds appear in the mythologies of Native Americans. In addition to the Pennsylvania region, they are prominent in the Indian lore of the Pacific Northwest and the Great Lakes region.

According to lore, thunderbirds shoot lightning from their eyes and make claps of thunder when they flap their wings. They soar through the skies on their enormous wings and sometimes swoop to the ground to snatch up children and carry them away. They dwarf the largest known birds: albatrosses have wingspans up to twelve feet and some condors have wingspans of ten-and-one-half feet.

Thunderbird sightings occur today. So far, only eyewitness testimony lends the creature credence. There are no proven photographs and no physical remains. No thunderbird has ever been captured, and no carcass has ever been found. Like Bigfoot, thunderbirds seem to slip in and out of our dimension.

Thunderbirds are reported around the world, but no place rivals the number of sightings in Pennsylvania. Most occur in the northern and western reaches of the state. The Black Forest, near the Ole Bull State Park, is one focal point. The Black Forest region encompasses Clinton, Potter, Lycoming, Tioga, Cameron, and McKean counties, all remote and sparsely populated state forest and game lands.

Here are some notable sightings in the state:

On June 13, 2001, a resident of Greenville saw a mammoth grayish-black bird, estimating its body to be about five feet in length

Spotlight on Ghosts:
Thunderbirds
(continued)

and its wings about 15 feet across. It landed in a tree, sat for a while, and then took off and disappeared.

On July 6 of the same year, another witness in Erie County saw a similar sight: a giant bird with a wingspan of fifteen to seventeen feet. It had little or no neck and a beak about a foot in length.

On the early evening of September 25, 2001, a giant bird was seen flying over Route 119 in South Greensburg. The nineteen-year-old witness heard a sound like "flags flapping in a thunderstorm" and looked up to see a bird with a head about three feet long and wings spanning ten to fifteen feet. It was about fifty to sixty feet above the ground and flapped its wings slowly and awkwardly. The witness watched it for about a minute and a half, and even saw it land in a dead tree, nearly breaking the branches with its weight.

Some contend that thunderbirds are real and not a paranormal phenomenon. Paleontological evidence exists for "teratorns," flight-capable birds eleven feet long and weighing 170 pounds. They had a wing span of twenty-five feet and feathers up to five feet long. They existed as recently as ten thousand years ago. Perhaps some survive today.

Ghosthunting
Travel Guide

Visiting Haunted Sites

Accomac Inn

The inn is located off Route 30 at Wrightsville. Take Route 30 east, exit at Wrightsville, turn north, and follow the Accomac Inn signs. The inn serves dinner seven days a week, and brunch on Sundays. Call 717-252-1521 for hours of operation and reservations. The Web site is www.accomacinn.com. If you are staying in the area, you can easily visit Codorus Furnace on the same day.

Alfred's Victorian Restaurant

The restaurant is at 38 North Union Street in Middletown. Call 717-717-944-5373 or visit www.alfredsvictorian.com/index.html. For information about Kelly and John Weaver's haunted dinners, visit the Spirit Society of Pennsylvania Web site at www.spiritsocietyofpa.com.

Baker Mansion

Baker Mansion is located near the intersection of Oak Lane and Crescent Road. It is open from Tours are limited to groups no larger than twelve persons, so book ahead in busy times of the year. Call 814-942-3916. You can take photographs throughout the house and grounds. Ask about special night-time ghost events, especially around Halloween. Visit the Web site at www.blairhistory.org.

Bolton Mansion

Bolton Mansion is located at 85 Holly Drive in Levittown. Call 215-943-6883 or log on to www.boltonmansion.org for information about public hours.

Bube's Brewery

Bube's Brewery and Central Hotel is located at 102 North Market Street in Mount Joy. Call 717-653-2056 for reservations and information. Bube's is lively and packed on weekends, so call ahead if you plan to be there at that time of week. The Web site is www.bubesbrewery.com.

Cashtown Inn

The Cashtown Inn is located at 1325 Old Route 30. The inn is open seven days a week and operates as a bed-and-breakfast. Call for restaurant hours; the restaurant is closed on Sunday-Monday. The Victorian Dining Room and the original Tavern Room offer delicious New American cuisine. Check the Web site, www.cashtowninn.com, for announcements about Civil War events and ghost weekend packages. Call 717-334-9722 to make reservations. The Web site is www.cashtowninn.com.

Chickie's Rock
To get to Chickie's Rock from Lancaster, take Route 30 West for 10 miles to the Columbia/Route 441 exit. Turn right onto Route 441 North. There are parking areas alongside the road.

Cordorus Furnace
Codorus Furnace is located on Furnace Road, off Codorus Furnace Road, about six miles southeast of Mt. Wolf, near the junction between Codorus Creek and the Susquehanna River, in Manheim Township, York County. If you have GPS, the coordinates are N 40° 03.122 W 076° 39.365. The ruins sit right off the road and are publicly accessible at all hours. The former furnace house along the road is now privately owned and off-limits.

Eastern State Penitentiary
Eastern State Penitentiary is located at 22nd Street and Fairmount Avenue, five blocks from the Philadelphia Museum of Art. It is open from 10:00 a.m. to 5:00 p.m. daily, except for Thanksgiving, Christmas Eve and Christmas Day, and New Year's Day. In the summer the twilight tours are especially popular, so call ahead at 215-236-3300 to inquire about tickets. The Web site, www.easternstate.org, offers an excellent history and overview of the facility and details about events and tours.

Fort Mifflin
Fort Mifflin is located at Fort Mifflin and Hog Island roads. Call ahead to verify hours of operation and activities at 215-685-4167. Historical tours are given during the daytime. Special arrangements must be made to participate in a night-time ghosthunt. The Web site is www.fortmifflin.us.

Fulton Opera House
The opera house is at 12 North Prince Street in Lancaster. For information on productions, call 717-397-7425 or visit www.thefulton.org.

General Sutter Inn

The inn is located at 14 East Main Street in Lititz. For information, call 717-626-2115 or visit www.generalsutterinn.com

Gettysburg

The Visitor's Center is located at 1195 Baltimore Pike, telephone 866-889-1243, Web site www.gettysburgfoundation.org. Mark Nesbitt's Ghosts of Gettysburg Tours headquarters are at 401 Baltimore Street, telephone 717-337-0445, Web site www.ghoststofgettysburg.com. You can find Mark and Carol, most weekends at their shop, where Mark is available to autograph his Gettysburg guide books as well as a superb field guide to ghost investigation in general. The Baladerry Inn is at 40 Hospital Road. Call 717-337-1342 for reservations. The Web site is www.baladerryinn.com.

Greater Johnstown/Cambria County Convention and Visitors Bureau

Visit the center at 416 Main Street Suite 100 in Johnstown for pamphlets, walking tours maps and other information about the Great Flood, the town and the ghosts. Call 814-536-7993 or go to www.johnstownpa.com.

Hotel Bethlehem

The hotel is located at 437 Main Street in Bethlehem. Call 610-625-5000 for reservations or go to www.hotelbethlehem.com.

Hotel Conneaut

Hotel Conneaut is located in Conneaut Lake Park, 12382 Center Street in Conneaut Lake, about two hours from Pittsburgh and about 40 minutes from Erie. For reservations, call 814-213-0120 or visit www.clphotelconneaut.com.

Inn at Jim Thorpe

The inn is located at 24 Broadway in Jim Thorpe. Phone is 570-325-2599. The Web site is www.injt.com.

Jean Bonnet Tavern

The Jean Bonnet Tavern is located at 6048 Lincoln Highway near Bedford, at the intersection of Routes 30 and 31. Phone is 814-623-2250 and fax is 814-623-2264. Or, you can email Melissa Jacobs at mjacobs@jeanbonnettavern.com. The Web site is www.jeanbonnettavern.com.

Logan Inn

Logan Inn is located at 10 West Ferry Street in New Hope. Call 215-862-2300 for reservations or visit www.loganinn.com. Adele Gamble's popular New Hope ghost tour leaves every Saturday night from the front of the Logan Inn. To make reservations for the tour, which is not associated with the Logan, call Adele at 215-957-9988 and leave a message.

McConnell's Mill State Park

The park is free and open to the public year-round from sunrise to sunset. The gristmill itself is open only on weekends and some holidays, from 11:00 a.m. to 5:00 p.m., from Memorial Day to Labor Day. Access to the mill is free and scheduled tours begin every hour. The state park is located about forty miles north of Pittsburgh off of I-79, near the intersection of Route 19 and US 422. For online mapping, or GPS, use 2697 McConnell's Mill Rd. Portersville.

National Aviary

The National Aviary is located in Pittsburgh on Ridge Street between West Ohio Street and West Commons. Call 412-323-7235 or visit www.aviary.org.

Nemacolin Castle

Nemacolin Castle is located at 10 Front Street in Brownsville. Hours are seasonal. From late spring to fall the castle is open weekends, Friday-Sunday, from 12:00-5:00. After Labor Day through November 1, it is open Saturday-Sunday from 12:00–4:00, and with special ghost tours from 6:00–10:00 p.m. There are nonghostly Christmas events, too. Contact the Brownsville Historical Society for specific information on tours, hours, and special winter holiday tours. Phone 724-785-6882 or visit online at www.nemacolincastle.org.

Old Jail Museum

The former Carbon County Prison, now the Old Jail Museum, is located at128 West Broadway in Jim Thorpe. The phone is 570-325-5259. Visit www.theoldjailmuseum.com for hours and special events. The museum is closed on Wednesdays. From Memorial Day through Labor Day, tours are offered from 12:30–4:30 p.m. The museum is open on weekends only in September and October.

Old Stone House

The Old Stone House is located at 2865 William Flynn Highway, Slippery Rock and is open on Saturdays from 10:00 a.m. to 5:00 p.m. and on Sundays from 12:00-5:00, May through October, and other times only for certain events. Admission is free. Call 724-738-2409 for information, or visit their blog at http://oldstonehousepa.wordpress.com for times and events.

Ole Bull State Park

Ole Bull State Park is located in Stewardson Township, Potter County, on Pennsylvania Route 144 (Ole Bull Road), twenty-six miles north of Renovo and eighteen miles south of Galeton. The drive along winding roads is beautiful, and at times lonely, taking travelers through remote areas known for sightings of UFOs and apparitions. Plan a full day to enjoy the drive and the park. There are plenty of places to picnic along Kettle Creek and lovely light hiking trails to explore. Camping facilities are available.

Pittsburgh Playhouse

The Pittsburgh Playhouse is located at 222 Craft Avenue. Call 412-621-4445 for ticket information. The playhouse offers performances from September through June, and is completely closed in July and August. Remember, there are no backstage tours, so the way to experience the ghosts is to attend a play and enjoy the entire ambience.

Railroad House

The Railroad House is located at 280 West Front Street, Marietta. Phone is 717-426-4141. Or visit the Web site at www.therailroadhouse.com for menus and events.

Riegelsville Inn

The address of the inn is 10 Delaware Road, Riegelsville, and the phone is 610-749-0100. Visit www.riegelsvilleinn.com for information about hours, events, and rates.

U.S. Hotel Restaurant & Tavern

The U.S. Hotel Restaurant & Tavern is located at 401 South Juniata Street. It is open for lunch Monday through Saturday and dinner seven days a week. A brunch is served on Sunday as well. Call 814-695-9924 for reservations. Ask for a booth in Dining Room 1, or a table in the Parlor, your best bets for catching a ghost. The bar also has a lot of ghostly activity. The Web site is www.theushotel.com. Also check the Web site of the Allegheny Mountain Ghosthunters, www.amghotshunters.com, for details about their investigations at the hotel and for news about their tours and events to the areas closed to the public.

Wayne Grave

Major General Anthony's grave can be visited at St. David's Episcopal Church in Wayne, 763 South Valley Forge Road. Look for it near the Old Church inside the cemetery near the entrance—it stands out as one of the largest headstones and is usually decorated with American flags.

Additional Haunted Sites

Tuscarora Academy
SR 3013 and SR 3008
Academia, PA 17082
An old school for girls destroyed by fire in the 1800s. Reports of little girls singing, crying, or playing. A black dog is said to haunt the graveyard next to the building.

The Ghost of Broad Street
Hazleton, PA 18201
A very tall ghost named "Pete" wanders the grounds of the Hazelton shopping center dressed in a hoagie shop uniform.

Hall Tower
1219 Old Willow Mill Road
Mechanicsburg, PA 17050
A fifteen-story tower in the middle of nowhere. Reports of a presence felt like being watched from the top. Some stories of voices inside warning to get out. Private property and off-limits to public.

Delaware County SPCA
555 Sandy Bank Road
Media, PA 19063
Reports of ghostly animal sounds and sightings after 11:00 P.M. Private property, no trespassing.

The Van Sant Bridge
Pidcock Creek and Covered Bridge Roads
New Hope, PA 18938
Orbs and mist seen in photographs. Reports of hearing horses galloping and feeling unearthly presences and feelings of being watched.

Allison's Grave
Mosquito Valley Road
Williamsport, PA 17703
Reports of a headless ghost named "Allison" haunting the cemetery causing feelings of dread and strange electrical activity.

Hanky Church Road
Hanky Church Road
Plum, PA 15239
The cemetery and empty lot across the street are said to be centers of spiritual activity ranging from strange sounds to glowing lights.

The Black Cross
Sasse Road/T618
Butler County, PA 16001
A large black wooden cross marks the spot of a mass grave. There is now a plaque and small cross to also commemorate. Reports of howling in the wind, orbs, and mist.

Livermore
Livermore Road
Blairsville, PA 17062
A half-submerged town and a graveyard on the nearby hill are reported to be very haunted. Full-body apparitions, orbs, and glowing eyes have been reported. The cemetery is restricted. No trespassing.

Gravity Hill
www.gravityhill.com
When cars are put in neutral on this hill, they reportedly roll up the hill rather than down.

Our Lady of the Sacred Heart High School
1504 Woodcrest Avenue
Coraopolis, PA 15108
Reports of a ghost nun that walks down the hall of the third floor. Private property; no trespassing.

Chestnut Hill College
Northwestern and Germantown Avenues
Philadelphia, PA 19118
Reports of strange happenings in many of the dorm rooms and surrounding areas.

Warren Area Student Union

330 Hickory Street
Warren, PA 16365
A ghost is said to haunt the basement. Flickering lights and an unnatural coldness are reported.

Old Torrance State Mental Hospital

Just off of Torrance Road, no address
Blairsville, PA 15717
Abandoned building with a mysterious history. In the basement, there is reported to be intense spiritual activity.

Woods Services

off Bellvue Drive
Langhorne, PA 19047
A house once used as a hospice during the revolutionary war, it is now an office building. There are reports of hearing ghostly footsteps, voices, and feeling strange presences.

Lorimer Park

Moredon Road
Abington, PA 17752
Apparitions and strange sounds are reported from this park. There is a pyramid in the woods said to glow on certain nights.

Northwestern Senior High School Auditorium

200 Harthan Way
Albion, PA 16401
A "blue woman" named "Lucy" is said to haunt the auditorium. The lights flicker and full-body apparitions have been reported.

King George Inn

3141 Hamilton Boulevard
Allentown, PA 18109
Ghosts from pre–Civil War era are said to haunt the Inn, especially the basement. Unexplained mischievous happenings are reported by the staff.

Bedford Springs Hotel
On Old Rt. 220 South
Bedford, PA 15522
Ghostly images are reported to appear in photographs of the hotel.

Covatta's Brinton Lodge
1808 W. Schuylkill Road
Douglassville, PA
Reports of footsteps on vacant floors and other mysterious occurrences.

Boling Springs Lake
N. Front Street and Mountain Road
Boiling Springs, PA 17007
A female ghost is said to walk around the lake at night and come to sit on a bench.

Snyder Cemetery
Burton Road
Butler County, PA 16001
Reports of cold spots, orbs, flashes of light, and strange fog among other things at this family cemetery.

Twin Tunnels
Creek Road
Downingtown, PA 19335
A suitcase full of dismembered female body parts was discovered under the tunnels. Reports abound of strange electronic mishaps and feelings of dread.

Forest Lawn Cemetery
1530 Frankstown Road
Johnstown, PA 15902
An apparition of a woman dressed in white is said to travel the cemetery grounds.

Erie Cemetery
2116 Chestnut Street
Erie, PA 16502

There are reports of feeling as though you are being followed in this cemetery. It is said that there is an apparition of a large black dog that will appear one second and disappear the next.

Old Main Tower at Mercyhurst College
501 East 38th Street
Erie, PA 16546
The ghost of a nun who committed suicide is said to haunt the tower.

Garrettford Elementary School
3830 Garrett Road
Drexel Hill, PA 19026
Reports of strange disembodied screams, doors opening and closing by themselves, and feelings of being watched or followed.

Edinboro University
200 Meadville Street
Edinboro, PA 16444
Lawrence Towers is reported haunted by the ghost of a former student. The elevator there experiences strange unexplainable problems.

Chiques Road
Chiques Road
Elizabethtown, PA 17022
An abandoned house on the road is said to be haunted by a homicidal father who killed his family. Strange lights appear and things are reported to move on their own.

St. Michael`s Church
Elizabeth, PA 15037
A church that was suddenly locked up and abandoned. There have been reports of orbs and strange mist in photographs.

Orphanage
Campbells Run Road
Harmarville, PA 15238
An abandoned orphanage, the road to which is closed off, is said to be haunted. Reports of strange flashing lights abound from the location.

Hotel Hershey

100 Hotel Road
Hershey, PA 17033
Mr. Hershey's ghost is said to haunt the hotel. Doors are reported to
open and close and strange sounds come from the cellar.

Lock Haven University

401 N. Fairview Street
Lock Haven, PA 17745
Paranormal events occur all over the campus. A white female apparition
is said to wander the grounds. There have also been reported sightings
of a Civil War soldier, as well as strange sounds such as the laughter of
little girls.

Malibu Dude Ranch

351 Foster Hill Road
Milford, PA 18337
Strange things are said to happen around the ranch. There are sightings
reported of a little girl apparition.

Carnegie Library

4400 Forbes Avenue
Pittsburgh, PA 15233
This library is said to have been built over an old cemetery. Spirits are
now reported to haunt the building.

Shawnee Inn and Golf Resort

River Road
Shawnee on Delaware, PA 18356
A female ghost is said to haunt the grounds of this resort.

Slippery Rock University

201 N. Main Street
Slippery Rock, PA 16057
Reports of a female ghost that haunts the auditorium and North Hall.
There is said to be strange banging and pounding, as well as the rattling
of doors and flickering on and off of lights.

Pennhurst State Hospital Complex
Spring City, PA 19475
A closed-down mental institution said to be heavily haunted. Reports of white apparitions, sounds, and presences felt. No trespassing.

West Chester University
700 S. High Street
West Chester, PA 19383
Several ghosts are said to haunt the university; they are most active around the school's homecoming.

Bibliography

Ellis, J.H. *Spirits in the Brewery*. Privately published, no date.

Fiedel, Dorothy Burtz. *Living with Ghosts*. Ephrata, PA.: Science Press, 1999.

_____. *Haunted Lancaster County Pennsylvania*. Ephrata, Pa.: Science Press, 1994.

Fisher, Rick. *Ghosts of the River Towns*. Columbia, Pa.: Fisher Productions, 2006.

Guiley, Rosemary Ellen. *The Encyclopedia of Ghosts and Spirits*. 3rd ed. New York: Facts On File, 2007.

Haunts of the Cashtown Inn. Compiled by Suzanne Gruber and Bob Wasel. Gettysburg, Pa.: Americana Souvenirs and Gifts, 1998.

Heindel, Ned D. *Hexenkopf: History, Healing & Hexerei*. Easton, Pa.: Williams Township Historical Society, 2005.

Lake, Matt. *Weird Pennsylvania*. New York: Sterling Publishing, 2005.

Macken, Lynda Lee. *Haunted New Hope: The Delaware Valley's Most Haunted Town*. Forked River, NJ: Black Cat Press, 2006.

McBride, Betty Lou and Kathleen McBride Sisack. *Ghosts of the Molly Maguires? A Decade of Strange & Unusual Happenings in The Old Jail*. Jim Thorpe, Pa.: The Old Jail Museum, 2006.

Motter, Leo. *Haunted Places in York County Pennsylvania*. Privately published, 2005.

Nesbitt, Mark. *Ghosts of Gettysburg*. Gettysburg, Pa: Thomas Publications, 1991.

Nesbitt, Mark and Patty A. Wilson. *Haunted Pennsylvania: Ghosts and Strange Phenomena of the Keystone State.* Mechanicsburg, Pa.: Stackpole Books, 2006.

Pavlik, Carrie. *The Ghosts of Hotel Conneaut & Conneaut Lake Park.* Third ed. Privately published, 2007.

Ramsland, Katherine and Dana DeVito. *Bethlehem Ghosts.* Gettysburg, Pa.: Second Chance Publications, 2007.

Wilson, Patty A. *Haunted Pennsylvania.* Laceyville, Pa.: Belfry Books, 1998.

Wilson, Patty A. and Scott Crownover. *Boos & Brews: A Guide to Haunted Taverns, Inns & Hotels of Pennsylvania.* Roaring Spring, Pa.: Piney Creek Press, 2002.

Acknowledgments

IN THE COMPILATION OF MATERIAL for this book, I was aided by people who shared information, their resources, and their experiences. Many of them are paranormal investigators I have known and worked with in Pennsylvania. In random order, I would like to thank: Tom Harter, founder of the Center for Paranormal Study and Investigation; Mark and Carol Nesbitt, owners and operators of the Ghosts of Gettysburg haunted walking tours; Rick Fisher, founder of the Paranormal Pennsylvania Society; John and Kelly Weaver, founders of the Spirit Society of Pennsylvania; paranormal investigators Craig and Melissa Telesha; Al Brinzda and Jon McLintock, founders of the Allegheny Mountains Ghosthunters; paranormal investigator Tom Long; Brian and Jennifer Shill, founders of the International Parapsychology Research Foundation; Brian and Terrie Seech, founders of the Center for Unexplained Events; Patty A. Wilson and Scott Crownover, founders of the Ghost Research Foundation; Adele Gamble, who runs the haunted walking tour in New Hope; Katherine Ramsland, author and paranormal investigator; Mick Retort, co-founder of the Watchful Eye Paranormal Society; Alfred Kirschman, operations manager of the Pittsburgh Playhouse; and Natalie Bock, historian of the Hotel Bethlehem.

About the Author

ROSEMARY ELLEN GUILEY, PH.D., is an expert on paranormal, visionary, and spiritual topics. She has written more than thirty books on a wide range of subjects, from angels to zombies and everything in between. She has written hundreds of articles for various publications, and is consulting editor for *FATE* magazine. Rosemary has had numerous experiences, from encounters with dark forces to mystical experiences with beings of light. She has been a believer in the unseen realms since childhood, when psychic dreaming opened portals to the amazing multidimensional universe. She says that our paranormal and spiritual experiences are undeniable, and have the potential to revolutionize every aspect of human life. Rosemary lives in Lutherville, Maryland.

Valerie A. Smith

Hop in and head out to other great destinations o

America's Haunted Road Trip.

Ghosthunting Illinois
by John Kachuba
ISBN: 978-1-57860-220-9
$14.95

Ghosthunting Maryland
by Michael J. Varhola and
Michael H. Varola
ISBN: 978-1-57860-351-0
$15.95

Ghosthunting New Jersey
by L'aura Hladik
ISBN: 978-1-57860-326-8
$14.95

Ghosthunting Ohio
by John Kachuba
ISBN: 978-1-57860-181-
$14.95

Ghosthunting Pennsylvania
by Rosemary Guiley
ISBN: 978-1-57860-353-4
$15.95

Ghosthunting Texas
by April Slaughter
ISBN: 978-1-57860-359-6
$15.95

Ghosthunting Virginia
by Michael J. Varhola
ISBN: 978-1-57860-327-5
$14.95

Hang on for the scariest ride of your life. Every book takes you to over 25 haunted places that you can visit yourself–or enjoy from the safety of your armchair. You'll find maps, directions, and dozens of photos, along with a hair-raising tale told by our savvy ghosthunters, who investigate each locale.

And be sure to visit us at americashauntedroadtrip.com
‹http://americashauntedroadtrip.com›

AMERICA'S
HAUNTED ROAD TRIP